May 2007

To _____,

Congratulations on your
College Graduation from
W. V. U. !

May God Bless your
future with love, joy,
and peace.

In Christian Love,
Wintersville Church
of Christ

Minister _____

Just for Today

GUIDELINES FOR LIVING

HAROLD J. SALA

CHRISTIAN PUBLICATIONS, INC.
CAMP HILL, PENNSYLVANIA

Published (2005) by
Christian Publications, Inc.
3825 Hartzdale Dr.
Camp Hill, PA 17011

ISBN 0-88965-253-8

Printed in the Philippines

To my friend, mentor, and inspiration,
Dr. Vernon Grounds,
whose quiet, humble way has given
two generations of men and women
preparing for ministry a model
and benchmark of excellence.

PREFACE

P<small>LEASE</small> G<small>OD</small>, <small>JUST HELP ME TO GET THROUGH THIS DAY</small>!"

Have you ever prayed like that? Sure, who hasn't? Forget tomorrow. Forget next week or next month; just help me to cope today. While the Bible makes wonderful promises that give hope for tomorrow, it seems to me that the greater focus is on God's help and strength for today.

Remember Jesus taught us to pray, "Give us this day, our daily bread . . . ."

He also told us, "Do not worry about tomorrow, for tomorrow will worry about itself. Each day has enough trouble of its own."

The Good News is that God's grace is always sufficient for today. That's what this book is about—finding God's strength and help for today!

My special thanks to Yna Reyes, who suggested that we compile short, encouraging selections from the many books OMF Literature has published over the years. Appreciation is also due to Beng Alba who painstakingly coordinated the project. I am also deeply indebted to my wife, Darlene; my daughter Nancy; and Casey Anderson for their editing skills. Apart from the indefatigable, competent help of Luisa Ampil, my friend and administrative assistant who cheerfully spent days typing and recompiling the selections, this book would not have happened.

I also want to thank you wonderful friends who say and write such kind and encouraging words and keep on urging me to give you "just one more!"

I am grateful to God for the privilege of sharing my heart with you. May God use this book not only to help you get through the day but to inspire you to make a difference in our world today!

Harold

EDITOR'S NOTE

DURING WEDNESDAYS, FOR MORE THAN FORTY YEARS, Dr. Harold J. Sala has been sitting down—first at a typewriter, then a word processor—to write the script for his radio program *Guidelines-A Five Minute Commentary on Living*. Selections from the 10,000 plus commentaries have found their way into more than thirty books published by OMF Literature. From several of these books he has selected 365 Guidelines he considers to be some of the most helpful and the best of a lifetime of speaking to our needs.

The books from which these entries have been taken appear in the bottom right hand corner. May God use this book to bring encouragement and strength to your life today.

January

IN THE BEGINNING
GOD CREATED THE HEAVENS
AND THE EARTH.

GENESIS 1:1

Embracing the New Year

Forgetting what is behind and straining toward
what is ahead, I press on.

PHILIPPIANS 3:13-14

*L*ike an emerging tender shoot through the barren
ground of spring, the New Year gives hope of something better to come.

There's a Peanuts cartoon where Charlie Brown says
to Lucy, "You're going to be proud of me, Lucy. I've
decided that this year is going to be my year of decision!
This is a list of the things in my life that I'm going to
correct. I'm going to be a better person!"

Lucy responds, "Not me. I'm going to spend the
whole year regretting the past. It's the only way, Charlie
Brown. I'm going to cry over spilt milk, and sigh over
lost loves. It's a lot easier. It's too hard to improve. I tried
it once. It drove me crazy!"

Are you holding on to the past instead of letting go
to grasp the present? Reread the Scripture text above,
and thank God for the renewal of His Spirit. You're on
the threshold of a new year. Make the most of it with
His help.

Tomorrow Begins Today

Just for Today, Lord

Give us today our daily bread. Forgive us our debts, as we also have forgiven our debtors. And lead us not into temptation, but deliver us from the evil one.

MATTHEW 6:11-12

*J*ust for today, Lord, help me live as though it were the last day of my life.

Help me see the blue of the sky and the green of the grass, the beauty of Your world as You paint the sky a thousand colors and shades.

Just for today, Lord, help me put into practice what I believe—that You are there when I need You, that You know me as I am, yet love me even when I mess up.

Just for today, Lord, give me the perspective of eternity, understanding that so much of what consumes my energy now will not count five minutes after I die.

Just for today, Lord, help me to get outside myself and my small world—my difficulties, my problems—and help me to listen to others.

This sounds like a pretty tall order, Lord, but this what I need. It's how You lived day after day, giving us an example so that we can follow in Your footsteps. And one more thing, Lord, please forgive me of my failures, shortcomings, and sin as I forgive those who sin against me. That's it, Lord, just for today.

365 Guidelines for Daily Living

Fifteen Minutes a Day

My people are destroyed from lack of knowledge
. . . because you have ignored the law of your
God, I also will ignore your children.

HOSEA 4:6

Have you ever read through the Bible from cover to cover? "Well, that would take a long, long time," you may be thinking. Not so long really. If you are an average reader, and took just fifteen minutes a day to read, you could read four to five chapters a day. At this rate, in eight months, you could finish reading the Bible—from Genesis to Revelation.

"I look upon it as a lost day when I have not had a good time over the Word of God," so commented George Müller who was an extremely busy man, yet found time to read the Bible through more than one hundred times in his lifetime.

Why bother reading this Book? Because no other book in the world will introduce you to God. If you want to know Him, read the Book. Remember, just fifteen minutes a day will put you through this Book in a year. It's well worth the time.

365 Guidelines for Daily Living

God is Bigger Than What He Has Made

Lift up your eyes on high, and behold who hath created these things.

ISAIAH 40:26 KJV

*W*ould it be fair to say that the true measure of a person is his accomplishment? For example, James Michener was considered great because of the books that came from his typewriter. The Sistine Chapel and sculptures such as *The Boy David* and *La Pieta* are synonymous with the excellence of Michelangelo.

We tend to judge an individual by his accomplishment. But Michener is greater than his novels and Michelangelo is greater than his paintings and sculpture. This being true, God has to be far greater than what He has created.

If God is bigger than His creation, then how big is He? We can't even figure out how large the universe is. There is one thing that I know though: God is infinitely larger than any challenge, any problem that shall confront me. When I realize that I am part of His creation, then I have to reach out by faith and say, "Thank You, God, that You are bigger than my need."

Tomorrow Begins Today

Can You Trust Your Conscience?

Having faith and a good conscience, which some having rejected, concerning the faith have suffered shipwreck.

1 TIMOTHY 1:19 *NKJV*

Have you ever wondered why one person can do something with apparently no conscience, while another person would struggle while doing the same thing? Does one person's conscience allow what someone else's conscience condemns?

If you can get away with sin, does that make it okay? Many people would say "yes." The fact is that your conscience is only as good as your knowledge of right and wrong. Can a person actually be guilty of something and have no feelings of remorse or a troubled conscience? Definitely. But when you know that what you have done is wrong before God, then your conscience becomes activated.

An understanding of how God wants you to live is the only thing in the world that will give your conscience the data it needs to be trustworthy and accurate.

The bottom line is not what you think, or what your culture will allow, but what God says. He has the final word in determining right and wrong.

Today Can Be the Best Day of Your Life

What is God Like?

In the beginning was the Word, and the Word was with God, and the Word was God.

JOHN 1:1

child's approach to God must have something of heaven intertwined in it. No wonder Jesus said, "I tell you the truth, anyone who will not receive the kingdom of God like a little child will never enter it" (Mark 10:15).

When my son, Steven, was about five years old, I took him with me to San Francisco. As I was negotiating rush-hour traffic, I wasn't carrying on much of a conversation. Suddenly, without any prologue, Steve blurted out to me, "Daddy, what is God like?" His question caught me off guard.

What is God like? I fumbled for words, trying to satisfy the curiosity of a little boy. I explained that, unlike us, God was never born. He has always existed and always will exist. I said that God loves us very much, so much that He sent His Son to give us eternal life; that God is faithful and just. He is always the same and never changes or grows old. He can always be counted on.

Make getting to know God a priority in your life.

Tomorrow Can Be Beautiful

Keep on Keeping On

Let us not become weary in doing good, for at the proper time we will reap a harvest if we do not give up."

GALATIANS 6:9

Discouragement is one of the world's oldest maladies. It seems that more people are fighting discouragement today than ever before. When you are tired and discouraged and feel like quitting because your good cause has been met with great oppression and apathy, first ask, "Was I fighting for the right cause?"

Second, ask yourself this question: "If I quit, who will take up the sword in the fight for right?" If you must re-think your strategy, fall back and regroup, strengthen the ranks, but do not quit. To win, you've got to keep on fighting.

Finally, ask one more question, "If I cease to stand for right, how can I expect weaker individuals to take up the fight?" At this point, you must not underestimate your potential.

Years ago, I wrote the words of Edward Everett Hale on the flyleaf of my Bible: "I am the only one, but still I am one. I cannot do everything, but still I can do something. And because I cannot do everything, I will not refuse to do something that I can do."

Today Can Be the Best Day of Your Life

Am I Really Responsible?

*Remember your Creator in the days of your youth.
. . . Fear God and keep his commandments for
this is the whole duty of man.*

ECCLESIASTES 12:1, 13

Can anybody really help the way he or she is? People are not born with equal physical and emotional strength. Just as some inherit strong physical bodies, others inherit stronger wills and personalities. A growing amount of scientific evidence traces a biological link between some of our emotional problems and our parents.

Some of us inherit a disposition from our parents that makes us more susceptible to destructive behavior. But does that excuse the alcoholic from wreaking havoc on the highway? Or excuse the murderer who says he is not responsible for the crime because he grew up in the slums and never knew the love of a parent?

With God's help, we can all change. You may require a lot of help and compassion from those who are close to you, but change is the door to hope and life. Don't ever let yourself think, "I can't help the way I am," because you can—with God's help and the help of those around you.

Today Can Be the Best Day of Your Life

Prayer in the 21st Century

In everything by prayer and supplication with thanksgiving let your requests be made known to God.

PHILIPPIANS 4:6 NASB

*A*lfred Lord Tennyson once wrote, "More things are wrought by prayer than this world ever dreams of." And the skeptic adds, "Yes, but that was more than a century ago—long before the advent of the 21st Century."

It's true, ours is a different world than Tennyson's. Yet it's just as true that the need for discovering the power of prayer is as great, if not greater, than a century ago. God was and continues to be our only hope.

Just what is prayer? Simply, it's conversation between you and God. But you've probably listened to someone pray in a beautiful ministerial voice, one that filled the sanctuary with flowery eloquence, and you said, "I can't pray like that. I guess I'll just leave prayer up to the ones who get paid to do it."

But prayer isn't superlative eloquence. Prayer is merely opening your heart to God and expressing yourself to Him. Prayer is intimate, meaningful talk between you and your Creator. If you haven't tried it before, why not start now by thanking Him for the blessings He has showered on you this day?

Today Can Be Different

How Far Can You Reach?

The poor you will always have with you, and you can help them any time you want. But you will not always have me. She did what she could. . .

MARK 14:7-8

There is a myth today that the needs of the world are so great that people would often say to themselves, "I am so helpless and insignificant that I can do nothing to make a difference."

This myth must be countered by asking two questions: "What do I have in my hand?" and "What is the reach of my arm?"

Actually, you have three things in your grasp: (1) time, (2) talents and abilities, and (3) resources.

The second question, "What is the reach of my arm?" is what gets you started. It is amazing what people who do not know what they cannot do are able to accomplish when they do what they can.

What needs in your neighborhood are within walking distance of where you live, within reach of your wallet or checkbook? Most lasting works of charity were started by one individual who saw a need and met that need. When the disciples objected to a woman anointing Jesus' feet with perfume, Jesus responded, "She did what she could" (Mark 14:8).

Dare we do less?

365 Guidelines for Daily Living

The Full Extent of Forgiveness

Be kind and compassionate to one another, forgiving each other, just as in Christ God forgave you.

EPHESIANS 4:32

*A*fter I spoke on the importance of forgiveness, a woman told me about the brutal murder of her son. He had been cut down in the prime of life, and she was angry. Even though the young man who had killed her son was already sent to prison, her heart was still filled with rage. As a Christian, she knew that she had to forgive, but she just couldn't do it.

"That kid in prison doesn't know about God," she thought. Eventually, she sent him a Bible along with a long letter, explaining how she felt. She told him that God, the Author of forgiveness, would also forgive him.

"Don't do this," the prison warden urged her. "You're wasting your time." But she persisted. "And when I did that," she said, "the burden lifted and only then could I forgive him."

Forgiveness is more than giving up my right to hurt you because you hurt me. True forgiveness means trusting God to handle the situation. Nothing else will do.

Tomorrow Can Be Beautiful

Take Up Your Cross and Follow Me

When they came to the place called the Skull, there they crucified Him, along with the criminals —one on his right, the other on his left.

LUKE 23:33

When Jesus talked about taking up a cross, undoubtedly some people slipped quietly towards the edge of the crowd. The cost was too high; the demands too great.

In today's world, what does it mean to "take up a cross"? Obviously, we can't take it literally, because we don't crucify people anymore. But the significance hasn't changed. Taking up your cross is an act of self-negation, a sacrifice, a commitment with a price tag attached.

Taking up your cross means caring for the elderly, feeding the homeless, sheltering the kids who sleep on the street. It can mean as many different things as there are situations, but every "cross" has the same significance. It means you have yielded control of your life to the Father. The power of the Cross transforms lives, and society as well.

May God help you to leave your burdens at His feet, take up your cross, and follow in the footsteps of Jesus.

Tomorrow Begins Today

An Inside Connection

"If you abide in Me, and My words abide in you, ask whatever you wish and it shall be done for you."

JOHN 15:7 NASB

ave you ever wished you had an inside connection with God?

In the Upper Room, immediately before He faced the cross, Jesus told the disciples, "If you remain in me, and my words remain in you, ask whatever you wish, and it will be given you" (John 15:7). That's a connection that must be honored!

Have you ever asked yourself why God should honor your prayers? Because you are a nice person? Because you are a lot better than your neighbor or the workers in your office? No! There is but one reason. You are a child of God, adopted into His family as the result of faith in Jesus Christ. Scripture tells us this very clearly. Galatians 4:6 says, "Because you are sons, God sent the Spirit of His Son into your hearts, the Spirit who calls out, 'Abba, Father.'"

The next time you are standing in the line of doubt and concern, wondering if God really hears and answers prayer, remember that you have an inside connection, one that must be honored.

Today Can Be the Best Day of Your Life

Forgiven

Father, forgive them, for they do not know what they are doing.

LUKE 23:34

*F*orgiven! No word in all the English language quite speaks to the heart as does this one word. To forgive means you are willing to give up your right to redress or to compensate for the wrong that has been done to you. True forgiveness puts the deed aside as though it was never done.

Because God has forgiven us, we have no right to refuse to forgive others and ourselves as well.

When the widow of a country doctor looked over the books of her deceased husband, she discovered that he had written "Forgiven—too poor to pay" across the page of many who owed him large sums of money. She, not having the grace to forgive so much, went to court to collect. The judge threw out the case. "What has been forgiven in the doctor's own handwriting," he declared, "cannot be collected by another." When the righteous Judge of the Universe forgives us, what right have we to try to make another pay?

365 Guidelines for Daily Living

When Things aren't Going Very Well

*And if we know that He hears us—whatever we ask
—we know that we have what we asked of Him.*

1 JOHN 5: 15

On the dark hours of the night, it's easy to begin to lose faith, to wonder if God really cares about you. Does it make any difference to Him whether you go under, or your business turns the corner and succeeds? Doubt creeps in and you say, "Maybe God doesn't care about me."

Malcolm Muggeridge said that atheists are the only ones on Earth who have no doubts. "The moment one believes," he said, "one automatically doubts, doubt being an integral part of faith."

When it is hardest to pray, that's when you need to pray the hardest. It doesn't always change the circumstances, but it changes the hearts of those who pray. Fight doubt by taking a Bible and marking the many promises of God. Put a notebook in the back of your Bible and begin to jot down dates and prayer requests, and then record how God answers.

Don't believe all your doubts and refuse to doubt all your beliefs. "Let God be true, and every man a liar" (Romans 3:4).

Tomorrow Begins Today

Grace — the Answer to My Need

Let us then approach the throne of grace with confidence, so that we may receive mercy and find grace to help us in our time of need.

HEBREWS 4:16

*G*race is God's generous response to the needs of your life. It is His provision for all that you lack, the answer to the pain and loneliness of your life. It is the vehicle of God's love that touches your life at the greatest point of neediness.

What is the need you face right now—food, clothing, healing, forgiveness, or companionship? God responds to our needs not because we deserve His help or favor. It is because of God's generous nature, which allows Him to do what we find almost impossible to understand. What God does is so foreign to what we would do if we were in His place. Our old nature says, "Why should I treat the beggar at my door with kindness? He hasn't done anything for me."

Grace is one beggar telling another beggar where to find free food and lodging. But in reality, grace is not free. God demanded that someone pay. That someone was the very Son of God, who became sin for us that we might receive God's free gift of salvation.

Today Can Be the Best Day of Your Life

Is There Hope?

*Be strong and take heart, all you who hope
in the LORD.*

PSALM 31:24

"Is there any hope?" This is the question on the minds of many today, not just of pessimists who are convinced that doomsday is just around the corner. It is the question that comes from thoughtful people who look at the increasing national debt, worsening AIDS epidemic, and the difficulty of keeping a marriage together. They are the ones who look at children growing up without even one parent.

Apart from a knowledge of the last chapter of the Bible, there would be little hope for us. But I've read this chapter and discovered that God is not disinterested in our personal lives. There is no problem so big or circumstance so difficult that God cannot turn it around. This kind of assurance gives us great hope for the future.

Are you hopeless and think your life is no longer worth the fight? There is good news. Life can be worth living. No matter where you are, no matter how hopeless the circumstances that confront you, read that last chapter. You will discover in the Bible that there is hope for your personal life and hope for tomorrow.

Today Can Be the Best Day of Your Life

Getting It Out of Your System

Let all bitterness and wrath and anger and clamor and slander be put away from you, along with all malice.

EPHESIANS 4:31 NASB

Negative emotions like fear, hatred, and anger are poison that can shorten your life. A doctor of internal medicine at Mayo Clinic contends that he has encountered many situations when bitterness or hatred was what actually caused the patient's illness that eventually led to death.

But how do we get the negative feelings out of our systems without allowing ourselves to explode in the process? When some are confronted with anger or dislike, they just get up, walk out and decide not to discuss it with the other person anymore, but the feelings are still there. There is another way, and that is to talk it out of your system by conversation with others—and in prayer to God.

When you pray, open your heart and let the emotions flow. Are you angry? Then tell God so in no uncertain terms. There is a logic to prayer that may baffle the scientists, but it works.

Today Can Be Different

The Prince and Pauper

I have been crucified with Christ and I no longer live, but Christ lives in me.

GALATIANS 2:20

Mark Twain's *The Prince and the Pauper* tells of two boys approximately the same age who were almost identical in appearance. One boy was the son of the king and the other was the son of a pauper. The two boys met and decided to exchange places. But underneath the story lies a truth of vastly greater significance than the boys' exchanged lives.

In similar fashion, Jesus Christ came to earth, leaving His position at the right hand of the Father. He temporarily exchanged His heavenly position as He came to earth and lived with the reality of sickness, misery, and despair.

The good news is simply this: Christ exchanged His life and place for us. He bore our sins in His own body when He died on the cross. By virtue of His death, God imputes to us the righteousness of Christ. What a paradox!

Christ was a prince who became a pauper. You were once a pauper and now a child of the King because of Christ's love for you.

Today Can Be Different

When You Need Help

*Cast all your anxiety on him because he cares
for you.*

1 PETER 5:7

here is an adage that goes, "Laugh, and the world
laughs with you; cry, and you cry alone." When
things are going well, there are plenty of friends to help
you celebrate your success. But when things take a bad
turn, you often discover who your real friends are.

Years ago, Paul wrote, "Bear ye one another's
burdens and so fulfill the law of Christ" (Galatians 6:2
KJV). Picture the image of a cross, for it was at the cross
that Christ died to bring mankind together, when we
had all turned and gone our own ways. He bore our
burdens there and, following His example, we are to
bear each other's burdens.

Also, in bearing each other's burdens, we learn to
cast our own burdens on a Savior who loves us and gave
Himself for us. Peter wrote, "Cast all your anxiety on
Him because He cares for you" (1 Peter 5:7). Bearing
each other's burdens helps us laugh with each other
and helps us avoid crying alone.

Today Can Be the Best Day of Your Life

The Image of the Father

For those God foreknew he also predestined to be
conformed to the likeness of His Son, that he
might be the firstborn among many brothers.

ROMANS 8:29

My grandson Andrew was a one-year-old whose smiling face was framed by a few brand-new teeth, a little bit of fuzz on his head, and glasses to correct a vision problem.

I was pushing him in the swing one day when a little boy looked at us and said, "You wanna know something? You guys kinda look alike!" "How's that?" I asked. His reply? "You both got glasses, and you both haven't got much hair."

While the observations of the little boy may have been superficial, I got to thinking about what he said in relation to our heavenly Father.

As God's children we also should take on his character as well as His likeness. In his first letter, John wrote that God's children have the remarkable ability to love—an ability that comes through a renewed relationship with the Father. "We know that we have passed from death to life," says John, "because we love our brothers."

I liked it when an observer felt my grandson looked like me. I think God smiles too when others see His characteristics in us.

365 Guidelines for Daily Living

Response to Trials

And we know that in all things God works for the good of those who love him, who have been called according to his purpose.

ROMANS 8:28

ne of the strange things about trials is this: When they knock at our door or sneak through the back door, we never quite expect them. When we struggle to overcome them, we often feel that nobody else has ever faced the same kind of testing.

The Greek word translated "testing" has two meanings: (1) a trial that comes from without, and (2) a temptation to do wrong that comes from within.

Periods of testing come to all of God's children. Long ago, Paul warned against presumptuousness or the thinking that you are immune from trials. He also assured us that when we face periods of difficulty, God will take us through. You will find those words of counsel in 1 Corinthians 10:12-13: "So, if you think you are standing firm, be careful that you don't fall! No temptation has seized you except what is common to man. And God is faithful; he will not let you be tempted beyond what you can bear. But when you are tempted, he will also provide a way out so that you can stand up under it."

Today Can Be the Best Day of Your Life

Goals for Success

I am the vine; you are the branches. If a man remains in me and I in him, he will bear much fruit; apart from me you can do nothing.

JOHN 15:5

century ago, the famous Harvard philosopher Wiliam James wrote, "Do everyday or two something for no other reason than that you would rather *not* do it."

Most of the time we take the road of least resistance, the broad road to mediocrity. The narrow road to excellence is uphill all the way.

Ask yourself three questions about your goals. The first question is simple: Are my goals right? A right goal is one that is framed in the perspective of eternity.

The second question is crucial: Are my goals pleasing to God? If your goals cut God out of your life, then re-evaluate them while you can still do something about them.

The third question is important: Assuming that my goals are right, do I have the patience to stay with my goals until they are accomplished?

Remember Paul's words, "I can do all things through Him who strengthens me" (Philippians 4:13).

In God's strength, Paul could—and so can you!

Today Can Be Different

Temptation

When tempted, no one should say, "God is tempting me." For God cannot be tempted by evil, nor does he tempt anyone; but each one is tempted when, by his own evil desire, he is dragged away and enticed.

JAMES 1:13-14

On the 1800's during the heyday of British shipping, greedy owners often overloaded their vessels, causing extreme danger to the sailors on board. One man—Samuel Plimsoll—became concerned and started campaigning against it.

Finally, the British Parliament passed legislation demanding that a line be drawn on the outside of every vessel. When the ship was loaded so that the water came up to that line, no more cargo could be brought aboard. The line became known as the Plimsoll Line, and Plimsoll has gone down in history as the sailor's friend.

God has also drawn a "Plimsoll Line" around all who put their trust in Him. "God is faithful; he will not let you be tempted beyond what you can bear" (1 Corinthians 10:13).

God may allow your character to be polished by trials, as wood might be smoothed by a carpenter using sandpaper. But He is faithful and will not allow you to be tried beyond what you are able to withstand.

Today Can Be Different

Focusing on the Father

*If we know he hears us—whatever we ask—we
know that we have what we asked of him.*

1 JOHN 5:15

Ignace Paderewski was one of Poland's greatest
pianists. It is said that on the afternoon of a concert, he would go to the building where the concert was
to take place. Then he would inspect the building,
room by room. Finally he would return to the vacant
auditorium.

Then giving instructions that he was not to be
disturbed, he would sit in silence for several hours. If
anyone spoke, he would start the process all over again.
In this way the great artist allowed the music to silently
flood his soul. He knew he must have time to concentrate, allowing nothing to distract him so that the
music would eventually fill his heart, and the overflow
would enrapture the audience.

I have wondered just what would happen, if we could
quietly sit in God's presence until His presence filled
our hearts.

You can connect with God by praying—worshiping,
listening, meditating, and talking to Him. Time in His
presence always produces a melody in life.

Touching God: Guidelines for Personal Prayer

Recovering Your First Love

Yet I hold this against you: You have forsaken your first love.

REVELATION 2:4

Could the reality that we've lost our first love account for the fact that—

- Less than half the people who own Bibles ever read them?
- Fewer than one in twenty ever share their faith with anyone?
- So many Christian organizations are downsizing because they have insufficient funds?

What is first love? First love is that deep devotion to Jesus Christ, which resulted from knowing your sins were forgiven and that you were redeemed with the blood of the Lamb. It was the warmth of devotion you first had when you were converted, when you were so excited about attending Bible studies and worship services, when you read the Bible for "ten minutes" and discovered an hour had gone by.

How do we recover what we've lost today? The way back is found in these three words: Remember, repent, and return.

You don't have to live with lukewarmness or fear that you have gone too far to come back. God wants you to walk with Him. The fire can be rekindled.

365 Guidelines for Daily Living

Feel Like Giving Up?

Therefore, strengthen your feeble arms and weak knees. Make level paths for your feet, so that the lame may not be disabled, but rather healed.

HEBREWS 12:12-13

*H*ave you ever felt like giving up? A friend of Guidelines wrote saying that he had prayed about something, but God had not answered, so he was giving up on the whole idea of a personal, caring God. Everyone at some time or another feels overwhelmed by discouragement and is tempted to conclude the same thing.

The promises of God are fenced in by His faithfulness. When Sarah was ninety years old, fifty years beyond the normal age for child-bearing, she brought forth a son. By faith, Sarah miraculously received the ability to conceive.

Unlike men who make promises, or sign covenants and treaties that are often broken before the ink is dry, God will honor His Word. "The Word of our God stands forever" (Isaiah 40:8). Therefore you can stand on His promises, confident that He will never fail you nor forsake you (Hebrews 13:5). When trouble comes, don't give up on God. Rather, tie a knot in the rope of faith and hold on. He'll be there at exactly the right time.

365 Guidelines for Daily Living

Who Cut In and Tripped You?

You were running a good race. Who cut in on you and kept you from obeying the truth?

GALATIANS 5:7

Occasionally we get tripped by other people. But most of the time, we trip ourselves. We forget the reason why we are in the race, and we forget the rewards of the victory. It's tough to stay focused, but it's the only way to finish the race.

Paul was talking about this when he wrote to the Corinthians, "Do you not know that in a race all the runners run, but only one gets the prize? Run in such a way as to get the prize" (1 Corinthians 9:24).

Here are four guidelines to encourage you:

GUIDELINE 1: Keep focused on your goal.

GUIDELINE 2: Resist discouragement. It's never wrong to be discouraged, but it is fatal to give up.

GUIDELINE 3: Renew yourself daily. "At the proper time we will reap a harvest if we do not give up" (Galatians 6:9).

GUIDELINE 4: Rely completely on the Lord. If we leave God out of our lives, we will struggle in our own strength and lose the upward dimension that renews our faith and our hope. So keep running.

Today Can Be the Best Day of Your Life

Where is God in Times of Trouble?

When you pass through the waters, I will be with you; and through the rivers, they shall not over-flow you. When you walk through the fire, you shall not be burned.

ISAIAH 43:2 KJV

Where is God in times of suffering? When my Jewish friend asked where God was when six million Jews were cremated, I responded, "He was in the same place He was when His Son was crucified outside the walls of Jerusalem."

"Where was God when . . . ?" It's an old question. *Where is God in times of disaster? Where was God when my baby died? Where is God when war tears a nation apart and families are separated? Where?*

There are some questions that will never be fully answered until we stand in the presence of God, but to turn from Him in the day of trouble leaves only bleak despair. Christ never promised deliverance from all difficulties, but He did promise His presence in times of trouble. He said, "'Never will I leave you; never will I forsake you.' So we say with confidence, 'The Lord is my helper; I will not be afraid. What can man do to me?'" (Hebrews 13:5-6).

365 Guidelines for Daily Living

God and Miracles Today

And I will do whatever you ask in my name, so that the Son may bring glory to the Father. You may ask me for anything in my name, and I will do it.

JOHN 14:13-14

The twelve disciples experienced the supernatural as they saw Christ heal the blind and cleanse the lepers. He also caused the deaf to hear and the lame to walk. The religious leaders were convinced that God had the power. But it was unsettling for them to see God's power being demonstrated by Jesus.

Paul explained, writing to the Corinthians, "God was reconciling the world to himself in Christ, not counting men's sins against them . . ." (2 Corinthians 5:19). Paul's explanation was that God's power was manifest in the life of His Son, Jesus Christ.

What the early Christians had, the church today seems to have lost!

To His disciples in the Upper Room, the night before the crucifixion, Jesus said, "I tell you the truth, anyone who has faith in me will do what I have been doing. He will do even greater things than these" (John 4:12). Do you believe it?

365 Guidelines for Daily Living

Sing to the Lord

Come, let us sing for joy to the LORD . . . Let us come before him with thanksgiving and extol him with music and song.

PSALM 95:1-2

When people are in prison, they try to recall lyrics that give them comfort. Consider Paul and Silas, who sang in a Roman prison. "About midnight, Paul and Silas were praying and singing hymns to God, and the other prisoners were listening to them" (Acts 16:25).

If you were arrested and put in prison, what would you sing to comfort yourself? Have you memorized any Gospel songs or hymns that would bring you encouragement and hope?

We don't know which hymns were sung in the early church, but we do know that their hymnbook was printed and has survived. We call it the book of Psalms. The book of Psalms is full of admonitions to sing and worship the Almighty.

Take some old hymnals and notice in the hymns the simple devotion and marked focus on the holiness of the Almighty. Whether they are sung in English, Ukrainian, or Burmese, hymns are part of the legacy that brings us together and reflects our common heritage.

Today Can Be the Best Day of Your Life

February

He has made everything beautiful in its time. He has also set eternity in the hearts of men; yet they cannot fathom what God has done from beginning to end.

ECCLESIASTES 3:11

When You are Tempted to Believe

I know whom I have believed, and am convinced that he is able to guard what I have entrusted to him for that day.

2 TIMOTHY 1:12

Francois Mitterand, the late President of France, was an intellectual and an atheist. Yet, in the latter years of his life, he had a fascination with death and a desire to know what lies beyond the grave.

He had confronted the possibilities of eternal life but never seemed to embrace it. Toward the end of his life as he struggled with prostate cancer, when asked if he believed in God, he replied, "I don't know if I believe in God, but I am tempted to believe."

Can God be known with certainty? The Apostle Paul wrote, "I know whom I have believed, and am convinced that he is able to guard what I have entrusted to him for that day" (2 Timothy 1:12). Millions have found the same answer and have died with the certainty that God through His Son offers us life and peace.

What lies on the other side of death? This question will never be answered by rationalism, philosophy, or mysticism. The answer is found in the Bible. Don't merely be tempted to believe.

Tomorrow Begins Today

Recovering from Disaster

Blessed are those who mourn, for they will be comforted.

MATTHEW 5:4

Disasters are a part of life, the result of living in an imperfect world. Here are some guidelines to follow when disaster knocks on your door:

GUIDELINE 1: Vent your grief. It is not a sign of weakness to let tears flow. Tears wash away bitterness from within and purge feelings of resentment from our hearts. But there is a difference between releasing bitterness and rehearsing it. Some people hold on to the memory of a disaster, re-telling it time and time again.

GUIDELINE 2: Let others minister to you. People who pretend that everything is fine are only compounding their pain. The family of God is there to serve as a safety net, a buffer between you and the pain.

GUIDELINE 3: Refuse to be bitter. Disasters result in either bitterness or blessing, but not both. King David's life seemed to be an ongoing series of disasters. Yet, he could look back and say, "Before I was afflicted I went astray, but now I obey your word" (Psalm 119:67).

GUIDELINE 4: Rely upon the Lord for strength. When disaster comes, you can hold on to the Lord or foolishly blame Him. You can panic, or you can pray.

Today Can Be the Best Day of Your Life

Keeping Yourself Pure

Religion that God our Father accepts as pure and faultless is this: to look after orphans and widows in their distress and to keep oneself from being polluted by the world.

JAMES 1:27

The Christian in a non-Christian world has always been a misfit. You may be the only one in your office who doesn't laugh at off-color jokes or use cuss words. How do you survive without compromising your convictions? Three guidelines offer some insight:

GUIDELINE 1: Stand your ground. You can't escape the world, but you don't have to lower your standards to make others comfortable.

GUIDELINE 2: Renew your commitment to decency and purity. Pray for God's strength, then rise from your knees with renewed determination to walk in the light of what you know is right.

GUIDELINE 3: Refresh yourself periodically. Periodically we need the washing and cleansing of the Word and the Spirit.

When you commit yourself to moral purity, others who lack the courage to be morally upright will follow in your footsteps.

Tomorrow Begins Today

Praying with Confidence

Then you will call, and the LORD will answer; you will cry for help, and he will say: Here I am.

ISAIAH 58:9

When Jesus prayed, the disciples discovered that the words flowed out of His heart. He didn't wait to pray until He found a cathedral with sunlight filtering through stained glass windows, nor did He wait until the Sabbath when He went to the synagogue.

He prayed everywhere, and whenever there was a need. When the disciples presented Him with the little boy's lunch to feed the crowd, He lifted His voice in thanksgiving; when confronted with sickness and disease, He took control over it; when the raging hostile winds of nature threatened to sink the boat they were in, He prayed and calmed the seas.

No concern is too small and no need is so great that you cannot take it to the Lord in prayer. As the Apostle John has written, "This is the confidence we have in approaching God: that if we ask anything according to his will, he hears us" (1 John 5:14). And when we know that God has heard us, we can leave the rest to Him.

Today Can Be the Best Day of Your Life

How Knowing God should Change Your Life

Therefore, if anyone is in Christ, he is a new creation; the old has gone, the new has come!

2 CORINTHIANS 5:17

On the streets of Manila, dirty, brash, young entrepreneurs—called cigarette boys—dash between the cars, jeepneys, and buses. They compete with each other in selling cigarettes, candies, and gums. One such boy was struck by a vehicle and the contents of his display board were scattered on the pavement. In a moment, a man stepped quickly from the crowd of onlookers, helped the boy to his feet, and began to pick up the fallen wares.

Somewhat dazed and not sure what to say, the boy looked intently at the man's face and blurted out, "Is you Jesus?"

When your neighbors and friends look at your life, what do they see? When God touches your life, something should rub off: the mark of the Divine. God's attributes should be evident in the lives of His children. The image of the Father should, in some way, be reflected in the countenance of the son.

Making the Gospel attractive isn't accomplished by making it easy but by making it desirable and authentic.

Tomorrow Can Be Beautiful

Trusting God More

Trust in the LORD with all your heart and lean not on your own understanding.

PROVERBS 3:5

*F*aith means unconditional obedience and commitment. Yet sometimes we don't like God's direction so we seek an alternative. Here are five guidelines to help you trust God:

GUIDELINE 1: Learn about God. You will never live long enough to meet a person who can honestly say, "God let me down; He disappointed me!"

GUIDELINE 2: Become a student of the Book. In the Bible, you will learn about the nature and character of our God.

GUIDELINE 3: Commit yourself to God's will for your life. Until you come to know God's goodness, you won't entrust your future to Him.

GUIDELINE 4: Realize that the walk of obedience is one step at a time. When I was young, a friend of mine gave me good counsel when he said, "God's will is like a flashlight in a dungeon; it doesn't shine around corners or illuminate the next cave—it only gives you light for the next step."

GUIDELINE 5: Realize that with God's demand for obedience comes His commitment to protect and provide for you. With such assurance, how can we ask more?

Today Can Be the Best Day of Your Life

The Ongoing Work of Restoration

For God so loved the world that he gave his one and only Son, that whoever believes in him shall not perish but have eternal life.

JOHN 3:16

I will never forget my first visit to the Sistine Chapel. Michelangelo's paintings were profound, but they were dark and dingy. The grime of several centuries covered their beautiful tones. But by the time of my second visit, several of the world's leading experts have restored them; the paintings have come alive. The restoration and cleansing made all the difference.

Restoration does not come without a price. It's much easier to leave something alone than to work at its restoration—applying the right amount of cleansers, with the right pressure so as not to permanently destroy the original.

Spiritual restoration is so important that God sent His Son Jesus Christ to accomplish the cleansing and healing of the masterpiece that He has created.

No one is ever beyond restoration and reconciliation with a loving God. Regardless of what your conscience tells you, or what others may tell you, God considers you a person worth saving.

Tomorrow Can Be Beautiful

Jesus' Prayers were Different

"Father, I thank you that you have heard me."
JOHN 11:41

*J*esus considered prayer a vital form of communication that gave Him direction, guidance, strength, and power. Yet a closer look at His prayer life leaves us with the impression that our prayers are much different from His. For one thing, His public prayers were short and His private prayers were long. And His prayers were not addressed to those who listened, but to His Father in heaven. He prayed with certainty and assurance that God was listening.

Why not make a list of your prayer requests? As you pray, believe that God will hear you. You might also want to read Mark 11:24 and John 15:7.

Write down how God answers your prayers. You'll discover time after time that He does hear and answer. Nothing brings greater delight to the heart of a father than to respond to the needs of his child. It's no different with God.

Today Can Be Different

My Strength is Perfected in Weakness

And then he told me, "My grace is enough; it's all you need. My strength comes into its own in your weakness."

2 CORINTHIANS 12:9 TM

Where is God in relation to our greatest flaws? Some folks think that God just ignores our failings since He's busy running the world, but that isn't what the Bible says. He knows our flaws and our weaknesses. So how does He view them? While the Bible contends that we are responsible for our failures, the best news of all is that God says, "My strength is made perfect in weakness."

The word *weakness* can refer to a physical or moral weakness. You know what yours is; God does too.

God never forces Himself on you. As you pray, "Lord, help me overcome my weakness," He goes to work. His effort begins and your weakness ends with your invitation to let Him meet your need.

365 Guidelines for Daily Living

An Unchanging Hope

We have this hope as an anchor for the soul, firm and secure.

HEBREWS 6:19

A woman, struggling to keep her business from collapsing, wrote to me, "My problem is that I have lost hope."

When you feel there is no light at the end of the tunnel, you lose hope. And when you lose hope, what makes life worth living for you quickly vanishes.

Giving up hope is like slamming the door on God. It is the equivalent of saying, "God, my problem is greater than You are, and I don't believe You can help me."

Hebrews 6 talks about the hope that comes through a personal relationship with God through faith in Jesus Christ. The writer of Hebrews attests, "We have this hope as an anchor for the soul, firm and secure" (Hebrews 6:19).

How is it with you? On a scale of 1 to 10, how does your hope meter register? No situation is hopeless when God steps on the scene, for *hopeless* is not a word that is in the vocabulary of the Almighty.

365 Guidelines for Daily Living

Freedom from Fear

There is no fear in love; but perfect love casts out fear, because fear involves punishment.

1 JOHN 4:18 NASB

*F*ears are the most disruptive, destructive things we can have," stated a well-known medical doctor. From his expert viewpoint, fear is a killer. It stalks our world, murdering faith, ambition and optimism.

Psychologists have much to say about neurotic fears. Few, however, trace fear to its recorded birthplace in rebellious Adam who, having lost his security in God, laments, "I was afraid" (Genesis 3:10). Ever since Adam, man has been afraid. But we have been given another chance through Jesus Christ.

An elderly Christian lady, after having read that God never slumbers nor sleeps, turned off her light, saying, "If God never sleeps, why should both of us stay awake tonight?" Her fears were dismissed because she knew the Night Watchman was awake.

When fear reaches out and grips you, fear not. Remember that God is with you.

Today Can Be Different

Making Peace with God

Are you tired? Worn out? Burned out on religion?
Come to me. Get away with me and you'll recover
your life. I'll show you how to take a real rest.

MATTHEW 11:28 TM

Making peace with God is not much different than re-establishing any relationship that has been broken by misunderstanding or wrongdoing. Isaiah says, "We all, like sheep, have gone astray, each of us has turned to his own way; and the LORD has laid on him the iniquity of us all" (Isaiah 53:6).

Making peace with God begins when you acknowledge that you have gone astray. Deep down in your heart, you know that confession should not be too difficult. The second thing you must do is recognize the voice of the Shepherd. Jesus, using this very analogy, said, "I am the good shepherd." He also said, "I am the way and the truth and the life . . ." (John 14:6).

The final step in making peace with God is to claim Jesus as your Lord and Savior and begin to follow Him.

It takes about as long to make peace with God as it does to swallow your pride and ask directions when you are lost.

Tomorrow Can Be Beautiful

The Triumph of the Cross

*Christ died for our sins according to the Scriptures
. . . He was raised on the third day. . . .*

1 CORINTHIANS 15: 3-4

*A*fter a devastating typhoon battered Macao in 1825,
John Bowring, the governor of Hong Kong, came
to explore the damage. He found buildings smashed,
homes devastated, and almost everything in the terri-
tory ruined. All that remained of the cathedral, which
had borne the brunt of the storm, was the facade, with
its cross standing tall on the pinnacle. Reflecting on
this scene of destruction, Bowring later wrote, "In the
cross of Christ I glory, towering over the wrecks of time."

Nothing is more central to Christianity than the
Cross. It represents the best and the worst of humanity,
but through it God brings redemption and forgiveness.

Our culture substitutes Santa for the manger, and
the Easter bunny for the empty tomb, but every grave-
yard, and every obituary reminds us that Good Friday
and the Resurrection on Easter morning give us life and
hope beyond the grave.

I heard recently that the old Macao cathedral is
being rebuilt—a testimony to the truth that the gates
of hell will never prevail against the Church.

Tomorrow Begins Today

Living the Language of Love

"A new commandment I give you: Love one another. As I have loved you, so you must love one another. All men will know that you are my disciples if you love one another."

JOHN 13:34-35

A middle-aged Chinese woman who lived through the Cultural Revolution told a friend, "The Cultural Revolution taught us to hate one another, but when I saw Christians who lived in love and reconciliation, I was drawn to them."

The early Church understood how powerful love is. What they lacked in experience, in education, in prestige and in influence was offset by the fact that these disciples loved each other. When God touches a life, it changes. One of the first pieces of evidence of this change is a person acquiring the ability to love others, not only those whose culture and lifestyle mirror his own, but those who are not lovable at all.

In the Upper Room, before His crucifixion, Jesus met the issue head-on. He told His followers: "A new commandment I give you: Love one another. As I have loved you, so you must love one another. All men will know that you are My disciples if you love one another."

Today Can be the Best Day of Your Life

Jeremiah—the Prophet of Gloom and Doom

The LORD said to me, "Do not say, 'I am only a child.' You must go to everyone I send you to and say whatever I command you."

JEREMIAH 1:7

Jeremiah hated the limelight but was constantly in the news. He loved the simple life, yet his was often complex and confusing. He felt inadequate as a public spokesman, yet spent his life confronting world leaders.

When God called him, Jeremiah gave three reasons why he considered himself an unlikely candidate: (1) his youth, (2) his lack of eloquence, and (3) his lack of experience. Pretty good reasons, right?

When God says, "You must go," it's hard to argue, especially when His hand touches your life as it happened to Jeremiah. His was not an easy life. He was forbidden to marry. Those who should have been his closest friends—priests and civic leaders—were his most bitter enemies.

God promised to be with Jeremiah, and He kept His word. According to tradition, when Jerusalem was overthrown by Nebuchadnezzar in 597 BC, Jeremiah escaped to Egypt and kept on ministering. Lord, give us today more Jeremiahs—men who will stand and be counted regardless of the cost.

365 Guidelines for Daily Living

Going One-on-One with God

You will seek me and find me when you seek me with all your heart.

JEREMIAH 29:13

Going one-on-one with God is not something to take lightly. In the hour of confronting your need, you must know that God can be trusted. Jacob went one-on-one with God when he wrestled with the angel. Moses did the same thing when he pleaded with God on behalf of the people he was leading. Here are some guidelines for going one-on-one with God:

GUIDELINE 1: Come to Him in simplicity and candor, and throw yourself completely at His mercy. When you go one-on-one with God, be completely honest with Him. He knows your strengths and weaknesses.

GUIDELINE 2: Stand on the promises of God's Word. More than a few times in Scripture we read about God doing something big and important so that people will know that He is God. He still shows His power today.

GUIDELINE 3: Approach God on your knees in surrender and obedience. Once you have encountered God, like Jacob, you bear the mark and you will never be the same again.

Tomorrow Begins Today

When You are in the Valley

*Therefore, since through God's mercy we have
this ministry, we do not lose heart.*

2 CORINTHIANS 4:1

As trust in God really enough to take you through the dark hours of the soul? When your life is ripped apart by a bolt of lightning, your light suddenly turns to darkness, is God really enough? This shocking question penetrates the darkness when a tragedy happens—your loved one dies or your business fails.

When Paul wrote to the Corinthians, he talked about the losses he had sustained, yet he was able to say, "We do not lose heart."

The issue is not whether you or your circumstances win, but how you fight the battle and whose side you're on. When you are tempted to feel sorry for yourself or give up, stay focused on God and keep trusting Him. As David says, "Even though I walk through the valley of the shadow of death, I will fear no evil, for you are with me; your rod and your staff, they comfort me" (Psalm 23:4).

Tomorrow Begins Today

If You are Lonely

Why are you downcast, O my soul? . . . Put your hope in God, for I will yet praise him, my Savior and my God.

PSALM 42:5

Do you feel lonely and unaccepted by others? God made you a unique individual, and He designed your heart to have a God-shaped vacuum that only He can fill. Until this vacuum has been filled by God, through His Son, Jesus Christ, you will always be a lonely person. Here are some ways you can find total fulfillment in God:

GUIDELINE 1: Admit your need. Tell your heavenly Father that you are lonely and without lasting hope. Nothing ever happens between God and man until man is humble enough and willing to admit his need for God's help and companionship.

GUIDELINE 2: Put your total faith in Christ for help. He is *the* help that you need.

GUIDELINE 3: Keep in contact with Christ, moment by moment. This you can do through prayer and by reading His written word, the Bible. Learn how to practice the presence of Christ. He is with you everywhere you go. Find in Him the permanent cure for your perennial loneliness.

Today Can Be the Best Day of Your Life

Uniqueness of the Bible

All Scripture is God-breathed and is useful for teaching, rebuking, correcting and training in righteousness.

2 TIMOTHY 3:16

Over the years men have fought for the Bible, argued over it, some have even died for it. We've seen dictators ban it from their countries claiming it brought unrest. Others have tried to destroy it, yet it endures.

The Bible has endured because it is God's textbook for living. It is different from other books. It gives answers to some of the basic questions that trouble the heart. It tells you who you are, where you came from and where you are headed. It gives you a blueprint for purposeful living. It does away with the grim pessimism that grips so many today and tells us that in Jesus Christ there is hope for the hopeless.

The Bible says the key to living is found in our relationship with Christ. "I am the way and the truth and the life; no one comes to the Father, but through Me" (John 14:6). The Bible tells you how you can live forever and how your life can be different forever.

Today Can Be Different

His Man in Burma

And the disciples were first called Christians in Antioch.

ACTS 11:26

*J*esus Christ's man in Burma!" This was not a compliment but a term of derision, scornfully hurled at a missionary by the name of Adoniram Judson. He was 25 years old, his wife 21, when their ship dropped anchor in Rangoon harbor on July 13, 1813.

Upon Judson's arrival, a friendly customs collector advised him to get back on the ship and go home. "I know what I'm talking about when I say to you there is nothing for you here but heartache," he said. But even the king and the combined military forces of the country could not stop this determined young man from planting the cross on Burmese soil.

"Jesus Christ's man in Burma"—originally a term of scorn and derision eventually became a title of honor and praise. The life of Adoniram Judson convicts me of lethargy. What most of us think of as difficulty cannot be compared with what men like Judson have faced. Could it be said that you are Jesus' man or woman? Whose man or woman are you, anyway?

Today Can Be Different

The Honesty of the Psalms

LORD, thou hast been our dwelling place in all generations. Before the mountains were brought forth, or ever thou hast formed the earth and the world, even from everlasting to everlasting, thou art God.

PSALM 90:1-2 KJV

In English we call it the Book of Psalms, one of the best-loved books of the Old Testament. In the Hebrew these 150 selections are known as the *Hallal*, or *Book of Praises*. Our English term "psalms" comes from the Greek word *psalmos*.

In the Psalms there is honesty that cuts to the very heart of the issues of life. *Why do scoundrels seem to prosper and the decent, moral person seems to lose out? Why does God not step in and make right the score for those wrongly accused and slandered? How long will evil go unpunished?*

Every generation can relate to the emotions and feelings of those who wrote the Psalms. Only the hand of God could have painted such timeless pictures of our lives.

Read and memorize the Psalms. They are an endless source of inspiration, blessing, and wonder. In them you can see yourself mirrored in the lives of those who learned to praise and worship the Almighty.

365 Guidelines for Daily Living

Read the Psalms

Blessed is the man who does not walk in the counsel of the wicked or stand in the way of sinners or sit in the seat of mockers.

PSALM 1:1

A young woman was despondent over a failing marriage. Trying to encourage her, I urged her to read at least one Psalm every day. "Oh no," she responded. "I never read that book. I never seem to get deliverance from my problems as David did, and that bothers me."

She had missed the whole point. Although David and the other psalmists wrote about their hope for deliverance, they also wrote about the impact of what was happening to them, including their emotions of love, hate, fear, and frustration.

If you haven't spent time reading this wonderful book, you are missing out on something that can help enrich your spiritual life. In discovering the Psalms, you will find the strength that allowed the Jews of the Holocaust to go to their deaths quoting the Word of God, finding strength to meet life's ultimate test.

Thank God for the Psalms—for their richness, for their meaning, and for their vivid description of our lives today!

365 Guidelines for Daily Living

Curing the Loneliness of an Empty Life

Surely I am with you always, to the very end of the age.

MATTHEW 28:20

Is there a cure to the loneliness of an empty life? How do you fix a lonely, broken heart?

Dr. John Wesley Shouse tells of the time when he picked up a hitchhiker and initiated a conversation with him. The hitchhiker told him how he made going to rock concerts a lifestyle. Dr. Shouse said he was a Christian, and the hitchhiker asked, "What does it feel like to be a Christian?" Dr. Shouse replied, "Being a Christian feels like never being alone."

Shouse understood the companionship that comes through a personal relationship with Jesus Christ, who said, "Never will I leave you; never will I forsake you" (Hebrews 13:5).

Religions are usually based upon the premise that a person must do certain things to appease God. Christianity is not. Christianity is a relationship and with it comes companionship that can assure you will never be alone. Get to know Jesus Christ, and you will never have to be lonely again.

Today Can Be the Best Day of Your Life

Four Questions

So God created man in his own image, in the image of God he created him; male and female he created them.

GENESIS 1:27

*W*here do you find the answers to life's questions? You can shrug your shoulders and say, "There are no answers—eat, drink, and be merry, for tomorrow we die." Or you can turn to the Bible, which gives us guidance to find our way in a topsy-turvy world.

Former British Prime Minister Harold MacMillan once said that four questions face every person that demand answers and these are the following:

(1)   Where did we come from?
(2)   What is the purpose of life?
(3)   Is there life after death?
(4)   Is there right and wrong?

In the Bible you can find answers to all four. Scripture not only tells us where we came from but also gives us God's purpose for our being here. In His Word you find that the grave is only the beginning of life beyond. And clearly the Bible gives us God's precepts of right and wrong.

Bring all of your questions to Him and find that He has the answers to life.

Today Can Be Different

It's Not Enough

Then he said to them all: "If anyone would come after me, he must deny himself and take up his cross daily and follow me."

LUKE 9:23

Is it possible for a person to go to church, put some money in the plate, and even belong to a church and yet still be lost?

What are the marks of a true Christian? Are there identifying characteristics, some criteria that Jesus laid down by which men and women can measure life and know if they are really headed for heaven? I believe there are at least four: *commitment, conversion, confession,* and *change.* Let's ponder that first one—commitment.

Do you remember what Jesus said when He first called the disciples? Is it "If you join My church, you'll go to heaven"? No, He looked into the eyes of people and said, "Follow Me!" It was that simple. And they who followed Him came from many walks of life. Farmers, fishermen, tax-collectors, laborers, and businessmen comprised the motley crowd who followed Him.

Their response to His call: *Commitment.* They followed Him. Commitment means identification. When you have been in His presence, He makes His mark on your life. Commitment is your response to His call.

365 Guidelines for Daily Living

The Marks of a True Christian

I tell you the truth, no one can see the Kingdom of God unless he is born again.

JOHN 3:3

The four marks of a true Christian are commitment, conversion, confession, and change. Apart from these, I would have serious reservations as to whether someone has really begun to follow Christ. Joining a church, giving to charity, or doing good deeds doesn't make it to the list. The true characteristics of being a Christian relate to your heart and attitudes.

Let's focus on the second mark of a true Christian: *Conversion*. It means a turn-about face. Peter Marshall, who served as chaplain of the U.S. Senate, described it as a tap on the shoulder when you are going one direction, and you hear the voice of Jesus saying, "Come, follow me!" and you turn around and head the opposite direction.

Here is how Jesus put it: "Unless one is born again, he cannot see the kingdom of God" (John 3:3 NKJV). Being "born again" isn't an emotional experience, but it does affect your emotions. It is the result of believing in Jesus Christ and accepting the gift of life He offers to all men.

365 Guidelines for Daily Living

Confessing Christ as Lord

*Therefore, if anyone is in Christ, he is a new
creation; the old has gone, the new has come!*

2 CORINTHIANS 5:17

The third mark of a true Christian is *confession*. It means that you have run up your flag and that you have identified with His cause. It means you are no longer a secret believer but have openly acknowledged Jesus Christ as your Savior. Here's what Jesus said: "Whoever acknowledges me before men, I will also acknowledge him before my Father in heaven. But whoever disowns me before men, I will disown him before my Father in heaven" (Matthew 10:32).

The fourth mark of a true Christian is *change*. When you receive Jesus Christ as your Lord and Savior, the Holy Spirit comes to indwell your heart.

Would you say, based on the four marks of commitment, conversion, confession and change, that you are a true Christian? If there is any doubt in your mind, pray a simple prayer right now. "Lord Jesus, I want to follow You. I believe that You are the one who lived, died, and rose again. I forsake my sinful self and bow at Your feet. I believe in You and receive You as my Savior and Lord. In Your name, Amen."

365 Guidelines for Daily Living

Don't Let Your Hearts be Troubled

You will keep in perfect peace him whose mind is steadfast, because he trusts in you. Trust in the LORD forever, for the LORD, the LORD, is the Rock eternal.

ISAIAH 26:3-4

et not your heart be troubled," said Jesus in the Upper Room at the Feast of the Passover, "ye believe in God, believe also in me" (John 14:1 KJV). When Jesus spoke those words, there were plenty of reasons for His followers to be worried. He had just told them that there was a traitor in their midst. As Jesus took the Passover cup, Satan entered into the heart of Judas.

When Jesus spoke those words He was looking beyond the small group who sat around that table. He was also speaking to those of us whose hearts have been broken and crushed by grief. He was speaking to the young mother whose baby is stillborn, the wife whose husband is stricken with cancer, the childless couple who desperately want a child, the young person who can't get a job, the loner without a friend.

Believe that the words of Jesus are true that He came from the Father and died for your sins. Yes, believe.

365 Guidelines for Daily Living

Four If Not More

Let the peace of Christ rule in your hearts, since
as members of one body you were called to peace.
And be thankful.

COLOSSIANS 3:15

An Indian man asked missionary Sidney Correll, "How many wives do you have?" Correll explained that in his culture, only one wife was acceptable. "I think you could have at least three or four wives," the Indian man said, adding, "for you are rich. You could have four if not more."

"Oh no. I am not rich. I am poor," Correll answered. The man smiled and shook his head. "No, you are rich. Look at your feet." Correll's eyes dropped to his feet. His shoes were dusty and showed the wear of travel. Then he looked at the feet of his traveling companion. They were bare.

One dad, realizing the difference between riches and wealth, said, "You know, we are rich already, and someday we may have some money."

There is little correlation with what you have and how happy you are. Gratitude is an attitude. You can possibly identify a rich man by his shoes. But you can always tell a grateful man by his attitude towards life.

365 Guidelines for Daily Living

March

See!

The winter is past;

the rains are over

and gone.

SONG OF SOLOMON 2:11

The Hand of the Potter Within

This is the word that came to Jeremiah from the LORD: "Go down to the potter's house, and there I will give you my message."

JEREMIAH 18:1-2

When I was a boy, I visited the old Van Briggle pottery plant near my home. I recall watching with amazement as the potter took a lump of clay, put it on the wheel, and began to work. Almost as if by magic, a vessel began to emerge. As the clay took shape, the potter put one hand inside the pot to keep it from collapsing while he applied pressure from the outside to mold it and shape it.

I'm reminded of how difficult it is for some people to cope with outside pressure in their lives. When they collapse, they blame God—the Potter—for allowing too much pressure. But the problem is not that there is too much outside pressure, but that people have not allowed the hand of the Potter to work within.

The hand of the Master Potter within us is what keeps our lives from collapsing. The outside pressures of the world will always be there, but as Jesus said, "Be of good cheer; I have overcome the world" (John 16:33 *KJV*).

Tomorrow Begins Today

Knowing Who You are When the Winds Blow

Therefore, there is now no condemnation for those who are in Christ Jesus.

ROMANS 8:1

To get a handle on your true self-worth, you must understand how God views your life. Go back to the events on the original Good Friday—the infamous day when Jesus was crucified by the Roman soldiers outside the city of Jerusalem. Why was He there? And what does His death have to do with your worth as a person?

The only reason that God allowed Jesus to come to Earth and die was because He considered you to be a person worth saving. He created you in His own image, but sin hindered you from enjoying the kind of a relationship with Him that He intended. The cross of Jesus Christ is the balance between the overly inflated opinion that some have of themselves and the "worm mentality" that makes people believe they are less than nothing.

My old sinful nature destroyed the image of God in my life, but I also recognize that being spiritually reborn makes me a child of the Father. I know I'm not an orphan in the world.

Tomorrow Begins Today

Who Told Ol' Hammurabi?

*For the wages of sin is death, but the gift of God
is eternal life in Christ Jesus our Lord.*

ROMANS 6:23

ammurabi's law code was written about the time
of Abraham. It contains nearly 300 legal provisions, including such items as false accusation, witchcraft, military service, land and business regulations,
family laws, tariffs, wages, trade, loans, and debts.

A study of these ancient codes reveals some common themes: the value and worth of the individual,
personal rights that should not be violated, and prohibitions and regulations ensuring the safety of families
and property. Where did these ideas of right and wrong
come from? The answer can only be the universal law
of God.

God wanted you to know clearly what He expects
of you. That's why He gave us the Bible, which tells us
clearly what is right and wrong, and specify the consequences for wrongdoing. But the Bible doesn't stop
there. It speaks of mercy and forgiveness. The common
theme is that God sent His Son, Jesus Christ, who
became the penalty for our sin, so that we might be
brought back into fellowship with the Father forever.

Tomorrow Can Be Beautiful

Deny Him, Ignore Him, or Adore Him

In a loud voice they sang: "Worthy is the Lamb, who was slain, to receive power and wealth and wisdom and strength and honor and glory and praise!"

REVELATION 5:12

Albert Einstein not only reflected on the theory of relativity, but on the meaning of life itself. Einstein believed that there was a God, but that this God was unknowable.

Some people deny God altogether. Perhaps they think that their colleagues in the university or the hospital may think that they're anti-intellectual if they recognize God's existence.

Some people simply ignore God.

Some people adore God, falling on their knees before Him in adulation and worship.

When Jack Hayford was in Britain on a certain occasion and saw the pageantry and preparation for an appearance of the Queen, he began thinking of the soon-coming appearance of the King of kings. Moved with emotion, Hayford quickly wrote the words, "Majesty, majesty! Worship His majesty. Unto Jesus be all glory, honor, and praise."

Tomorrow Can Be Beautiful

Making Your Sick Bed Softer

For he says, "In the time of my favor I heard you, and in the day of salvation I helped you." I tell you, now is the time of God's favor, now is the day of salvation.

2 CORINTHIANS 6:2

On his sickbed prior to death, Charles Spurgeon said, "If you do not wish to be full of regrets when you are forced to lie still, work while you can. If you desire to make a sickbed as soft as it can be, do not stuff it with mournful reflections that you wasted time when you were in health and strength."

Here are four guidelines for living a life without regrets:

GUIDELINE 1: Plan it now. Some things you can't do now, but you can prepare to do them when the right time comes.

GUIDELINE 2: Do it now. Don't wait until you retire to start a hobby, take a trip, or remodel the house.

GUIDELINE 3: Say it now. Tell your spouse and your kids that you love them.

GUIDELINE 4: Live it now. Make your peace with God now, not on your deathbed.

Good advice to make your sick bed softer.

Tomorrow Can Be Beautiful

The Tremendous Power of Love

Whoever does not love does not know God, because God is love.

1 JOHN 4:8

No person can be a well-rounded individual and relate to the world around him if he has not discovered the power of love itself.

This truth is beautifully illustrated in the story of a female prisoner in Paris who was lonely, afraid, and bitter. She resisted any attempt to break through her barrier. A prison worker often spoke to her and tried to share God's love, but the response was a snarl. "Nobody loves me—don't talk to me."

Then one day, as the prison worker began her rounds through the jail, an opportunity came. As she passed the prisoner, without thinking, she bent over and kissed her. The prisoner reeled back and began to weep. "Why did you kiss me?" she asked. "Nobody has kissed me for many years. Kick me, strike me, use me and leave me—but kiss me, no!"

Don't give up striving to reach out in love when your attempts are rebuffed. And when people attempt to show love to you, realize that their love not only meets a need of yours, but it meets a need of theirs as well.

Today Can Be the Best Day of Your Life

Power to Become

But as many as received him, to them gave he power to become the sons of God.

JOHN 1:12 KJV

Years ago, in the highlands of Scotland, a rascal was caught by his neighbors stealing sheep from his friend. Incensed by his repeated thefts, the crowd yelled and cursed his name. Then several men took a knife and carved the letters ST—for sheep thief—on his forehead, an act that left an ugly scar.

As the man grew older, he converted to Christianity and his life changed drastically. Slowly, he was accepted in the parish church, and, eventually, his neighbors began to look beyond the initials carved on his forehead.

One day, a little boy asked, "Mama, what does that 'ST' mean on that man's forehead?"

Pausing for a moment, she replied, "Son, I think that means 'saint'."

There you have it—sheep thief to saint. Now only God can do that; He can and He does.

The good news today is that no matter how you have been branded by the crowds, God will receive you and change your life! "Power to become"—let that phrase grip your heart and life today.

Today Can Be Different

Getting Back on the Right Road

If any of you lacks wisdom, he should ask God, who gives generously to all without finding fault, and it will be given to him.

JAMES 1:5

When you have wandered the path of the prodigal, I suggest three guidelines for getting back on the right road of doing the will of your heavenly Father:

GUIDELINE 1: Admit your mistake. Saying "I have sinned!" or "I'm wrong!" is never easy.

GUIDELINE 2: Ask for help. The book of James says, "If any of you lacks wisdom, he should ask God, who gives generously to all without finding fault, and it will be given to him" (James 1:5).

GUIDELINE 3: Start over. This time, practice a measure of humility. You can learn from your failure and start again, which is good news.

Okay, you blew it, you failed radically, you sinned. But there is an awesome God, who is also the God of the second chance, and I could say, the third and the fourth. He is the God of unlimited grace. With His help, you can get back on the right road and head for home.

365 Guidelines for Daily Living

Be of Good Cheer

In the world ye shall have tribulations: but be of good cheer; I have overcome the world.

JOHN 16:33 KJV

*T*en times in the King James translation of the Bible you will encounter the phrase *Be of good cheer*. Seven times the phrase is associated with an impossible situation.

Paul was in a ship in a terrible storm when he challenged the circumstances, saying, "Be of good cheer: for I believe God, that it shall be even as it was told me" (Acts 27:24 *KJV*).

When the ship of your life is driven towards the rocks, can you say, "I'll keep up my courage because I believe in God!"? Here's how:

GUIDELINE 1: Go back to the Bible and claim the promises of God. They must be taken by faith.

GUIDELINE 2: Commit yourself to the care and keeping of your heavenly Father.

GUIDELINE 3: Commit to Him what you cannot change and ask Him for His grace and strength to not only survive but to conquer.

Gradually despair will turn to hope, and you will be able to say, "I'll keep up my courage because I believe in God." It's the only way to defy the despair of circumstances.

365 Guidelines for Daily Living

Why God Uses People

*And without faith it is impossible to please God,
because anyone who comes to him must believe
that he exists and that he rewards those who
earnestly seek him.*

HEBREWS 11:6

Some of the most successful leaders in the Christian
world initially have had little real promise of success.
God used some unlikely individuals such as the writer
of *Pilgrim's Progress* John Bunyan, who earned his
living as a tinker, which is something like a welder
today. Then there was Dwight L. Moody, the shoe
salesman who turned into an evangelist and helped
bring thousands to Christ.

Is it possible that God uses the less qualified individuals to do His greatest works because when individuals lack much, they also trust much? And people who
are gifted, educated, and have personal resources trust
their own abilities rather than Him who called them?

Long ago Paul wrote to a group of people who boasted
in their wisdom and education, "But God hath chosen
the foolish things of the world to confound the wise;
and God hath chosen the weak things of the world to
confound the things which are mighty" (1 Corinthians
1:27 KJV).

365 Guidelines for Daily Living

At the End of the Rope

*Do not be afraid or discouraged because of this
vast array, for the battle is not yours, but God's.*

2 CHRONICLES 20:15

He was at the end of the road, with his back to the wall. No hope in sight—at least that's how it seemed. An army of men was across the Jordan, 18 miles from the capital city of Jerusalem. Intelligence reports had failed, and the secretary of defense rushed into the capitol with the message that an invasion by the enemy was imminent.

His name was King Jehoshaphat, and according to 2 Chronicles 20, he quickly realized human hope was gone. But that was actually the first step in reaching God. We are independent creatures who scheme and plan and plot intrigue to solve our own problems. When we realize the problem is bigger than we are, however, then we realize that God can help.

The second thing that Jehoshaphat did was to earnestly seek God's help. He invited the people to meet together for prayer, and pray they did. God saw the worried king through his crisis. Jehoshaphat won the battle without firing a shot. So can you. Trust God.

Today Can Be Different

Knowing Him

*I want to know Christ and the power of his
resurrection and the fellowship of sharing in his
sufferings, becoming like him in his death.*

PHILIPPIANS 3:10

When Mark Twain returned from a world cruise,
he related his experiences meeting some of the
world's great people. His son, then a little boy, listened
rapturously and then exclaimed, "You know, Dad, you
must know about everybody except God." Unfortun-
ately, the exception makes the rest meaningless.

Certainly Paul knew Christ. But what he is saying
in Philippians 3:10 is that he wants to know Him more
deeply, more intimately, more completely. He wants to
develop an ongoing, deepening relationship. Can you
relate to that?

Don't be content with less than a personal knowledge of Christ. He invites you to Himself as He says,
"Come to me, all you who are weary and burdened,
and I will give you rest" (Matthew 11:28).

The Jesus that you grew up with, the One you heard
about in religious education, may well be different
from the One revealed in the New Testament. Get to
know the real Jesus. He'll change your life. Knowing
everybody but God falls short of the most important
relationship of all.

Tomorrow Can Be Beautiful

When You Feel Like Just Staying in Bed

Therefore do not worry about tomorrow, for tomorrow will worry about itself.

MATTHEW 6:34

There are days when you feel like you should have just stayed in bed. But you don't have that choice. Do you ever wonder if God is trying to tell you something? Have you ever considered the possibility that you need to back away from your situation and see it from a different perspective?

If God is sovereign—and He is—and if you are His child, then nothing can happen to you beyond His knowledge and will. Nothing? Yes, nothing. With that single word, we can turn the corner and face our human inadequacy and the greatness of God's resources and power.

God usually doesn't override my blunders, but He does give me the courage to go on and the wisdom to learn from my mistakes. He doesn't change the immutable laws of cause and effect, but He does lift me up and set my feet on a straight path.

When you have one of those days, don't take yourself too seriously. Remember, this too shall pass. Still, it isn't a bad idea to consult God about what lies ahead even before you rise in the morning.

Tomorrow Begins Today

The Great Barrier Reef

I can do everything through him who gives me strength.

PHILIPPIANS 4:13

He rowed alone across the Pacific Ocean 8,990 miles but fell short of his goal 33 miles away. Peter Bird attempted to become the first man to single-handedly row from San Francisco across the Pacific. He almost succeeded, but approaching the east coast of Australia's Great Barrier Reef, Bird encountered stormy weather and choppy seas. He was within one nautical mile of the reef when he had to radio for help from Royal Australian Navy.

Peter Bird did make it to Australia, but he had to have the assistance of the Australian Navy. In the same way, you will often need the help and support of God and others when life's storms are too difficult to brave alone. Maybe you have come a long, long way in your Christian walk, but you are discouraged and feel like giving up. Hang in there; help is coming.

The writer of the book of Hebrews encouraged struggling believers to get their eyes on the Lord Jesus—not on circumstances—as the Author, Finisher, and the One who completes their faith.

Today Can Be the Best Day of Your Life

Confronting Issues Graciously

Anyone, then, who knows the good he ought to do and doesn't do it, sins.

JAMES 4:17

When you are confronted with a situation you feel is wrong, follow these guidelines:

GUIDELINE 1: Talk to others in your community or peer group. Your concern may be the catalyst, which God can use to accomplish great good.

GUIDELINE 2: Pray about the issue before you do anything. This often helps you deal with anger and helps you channel your feelings productively.

GUIDELINE 3: Do some research. Find out what the law is or who is in charge.

GUIDELINE 4: Raise the issue without raising your voice. When one person objects to something, only a few people pay attention to the issue. But when thirty people object to the same issue, it gets attention.

GUIDELINE 5: Don't give up when you know that you are right.

Edmund Burke, the British patriot, said, "All that is necessary for evil to triumph is for good men to do nothing." Make your voice heard. It may be all that it takes to move others to take a stand for right.

365 Guidelines for Daily Living

What Drives Your Life?

For to me, to live is Christ and to die is gain.

PHILIPPIANS 1:21

Every person is driven by something. It could be the desire for money, fame, pleasure or success. Whatever it is, something drives a person's life. Do you know what drives your life?

For what purpose did God put you here on earth? Obviously God has a purpose for you. But until you bring God into the picture, you will never fully understand what life is about.

The following guidelines can help you bring the whole issue into focus:

GUIDELINE 1: Recognize what drives your life today.

GUIDELINE 2: Realize that God has a purpose for your life. You are no accident, no chance happening.

GUIDELINE 3: Receive the fullness of life that God intends you to have. "For to me, to live is Christ and to die is gain," wrote Paul (Philippians 1:21). He knew what made his life worth living. How would you define your life purpose? You have one. Find out what it is.

Tomorrow Begins Today

Suffering—Why?

Even though I walk through the valley of the shadow of death, I will fear no evil, for you are with me.

PSALM 23:4

Have you ever experienced a time when everything was going just right and then for no apparent reason everything went wrong? Whenever misfortune strikes, the question usually asked is: "Why? Why did God let this happen to me?"

The Bible gives us insight into suffering. Sometimes God allows us to suffer so we can slow down and take stock of our lives. It may be that you are now walking through an hour of darkness so that you will find God's Son as the light of your life. Jesus knew what it meant to suffer—he experienced physical pain, the loneliness of being forsaken by His friends, and the agony of facing death. While it is true that He lived a sinless life, He was still human and can understand your hurts.

The Bible says, "The LORD is good, a refuge in times of trouble. He cares for those who trust in him" (Nahum 1:7). Have you made the wonderful discovery of taking refuge in the Lord and trusting Him when trouble knocks at your door? Do not hesitate to turn to Him for grace and strength.

Today Can Be the Best Day of Your Life

Committing the Bible to Heart

I have hidden your word in my heart, that I might not sin against you.

PSALM 119:11

*Y*ears ago, during the days of the USSR, as I disembarked from the plane in Russia and entered customs, I was greeted with: "What kind of reading materials do you have?" I reached into my bag and produced a *Reader's Digest* and *Newsweek*. Browsing through them, the inspector asked, "What else do you have?" This time I reached a little deeper and pulled out my New Testament. When he called over several others, I asked, "Is something wrong? Don't you allow Bibles in the Soviet Union?" Caught by surprise, they quickly handed it back.

If by chance every Bible were taken from your home, how much of this priceless book would you retain in your heart? In my hotel room in Russia, I seriously thought, "Even though I hold a Ph.D. in biblical text, if I do not see a Bible for the next five years, how much of it would have stayed in my heart?" That experience made me realize the only real Word that can never be taken away is that which is committed to memory and translated into our lives.

Today Can Be Different

Facing Life with Courage

For you have been born again, not of perishable seed, but of imperishable, through the living and enduring word of God.

1 PETER 1:23

*W*illiam Carey of England was one of the pioneers of the modern missionary movement when he went to India. There he worked on translating the Bible into the language of the people.

One day, Carey returned to find that a disastrous fire had broken out, completely destroying the building. But far more damaging, his manuscripts, dictionaries and grammar books had all gone up in flames as well.

Did Carey react to this turn of events violently? No, he didn't. "Without a word of despair, impatience or anger," writes one biographer, "he knelt and thanked God that he still had the strength to do the work all over again!" After years of Carey's effort, Bibles were eventually printed and distributed.

Romans 8:28 says, "And we know that in all things God works for the good of those who love him." It doesn't say, "We think" or "we understand" or "we feel". Simply, "We know!" And with that confidence we must rest.

Today Can Be Different

Living in the Shadow of the Almighty

He who dwells in the shelter of the Most High will rest in the shadow of the Almighty.

PSALM 91:1

*L*iving in the shadow of the Almighty makes us invulnerable to our enemies. It means that safety isn't the absence of danger but the presence and protection of the Lord. The dwelling place of the Most High can be found wherever you meet God—your bedroom, your office, or your hiding place.

The Hebrew word that is translated "abide" or "dwell" literally means to pitch a tent as a temporary dwelling, or to bed down as you would in a cave when you were pursued by an enemy.

Today we desperately need to discover that place of refuge. The hymn writer spoke of it, saying,

There is a place of quiet rest, near to the heart of God.

A place where sin cannot molest, near to the heart of God.

If you have never found a "secret place of refuge," make one—the place where you meet God in surrender and commitment. Once you have been there, you will never again be content being anywhere else.

365 Guidelines for Daily Living

Overcoming the Enemy

*They overcame him by the blood of the Lamb
and by the word of their testimony.*

REVELATION 12:11

riting the last book of the New Testament, the Apostle John, one of the youngest of the twelve who walked with Jesus, describes a scene where there was a battle of spiritual forces in heaven. He says, "The great dragon was hurled down—that ancient serpent called the devil, or Satan, who leads the whole world astray. He was hurled to the earth, and his angels with him. . . . He is filled with fury, because he knows that his time is short" (Revelation 12:9, 12).

What's happening in our world today tells us that Satan's time is short. The day is fast approaching when God will say, "Enough is enough!" and send His Son to establish His kingdom, when people will beat their swords into plowshares and their instruments of warfare into pruning hooks.

Of the arch-enemy Satan, John says, "They overcame him by the blood of the Lamb and by the word of their testimony" (Revelation 12:11). When it comes to your own personal struggle with evil, you can win in the same way.

365 Guidelines for Daily Living

Compassion

Finally, all of you, live in harmony with one another; be sympathetic, love as brothers, be compassionate and humble.

1 PETER 3:8

*T*he *Washington Post* uses the word compassion as a synonym for governmental spending to help the needy and homeless. But this idea of compassion being a government program is a far cry from the biblical concept of the word. The term compassion, found some forty-one times in thirty-nine verses, always includes personal involvement.

Jesus is an example of this personal involvement. He personally reached out in compassion to the multitudes of people who came near him—individuals who were harassed and helpless, "like sheep without a shepherd." Peter said in his first letter, "Finally, all of you, live in harmony with one another; be sympathetic, love as brothers, be compassionate and humble."

You may be thinking, "There are a lot of hurting people out there. I can't help them all!" If, however, one hurting person crossed your path and reached out to you in need, could you stop long enough to hear what he or she hears, to feel what he or she feels, and to be there in his or her time of need? That is where compassion begins.

Today Can Be the Best Day of Your Life

A Bad News World

Like cold water to a weary soul is good news from a distant land.

PROVERBS 25:25

Have you noticed how little "good news" there is any more in a bad news world? It is not without reason that we refer to the Gospel as "The Good News!"

Firstly, it tells you that God is concerned with you. This is in contrast to how life today leaves you with the impression that there are few who care about what happens to you.

Secondly, it promises an end to the problems confronting the world. The Bible says that God is in control. Reading the book of Revelation reveals the eventual return of the Prince of Peace to rule and reign. It says there is a limit to how far God will allow humanity to go; He'll eventually step in and say, "That's enough."

Finally, it tells you that your life can be different. That is the best news of all. With God, there is forgiveness and help. You need not be a victim of your failure and sin or live in bondage to the hostilities that imprison. You can be a new person with a hope and a future.

Read the Bible. There you'll find the best news you will ever get.

Today Can Be the Best Day of Your Life

A Fool for God

God said to him, "You fool! This very night your life will be demanded from you. Then who will get what you have prepared for yourself?"

LUKE 12:20

Risk your money on dice, and people call you a gambler. Risk your money on the stock market, and they call you an investor. But risk your future on God, and they call you a fool.

Abraham, who risked everything on God, might have been thought of as a fool when he spoke of God's command for him to leave his hometown. Of his step of faith, Hebrews 11:8 (*KJV*) says, "By faith Abraham, when he was called to go out into a place which he should after receive for an inheritance, obeyed; and he went out, not knowing whither he went."

Men and women who walk by faith will always be out of step with their peers and will be "fanatics" who take the truth of God's Word literally. People of such faith have always been in a minority.

Every person's life makes a statement. Some people live for God, some for fame, some for power and influence. But Abraham lived for God. So his life's statement was "God will respond to the person who lives in faith."

What statement does your life make?

Today Can Be Different

Dropping the "A" from Atheism

The fool says in his heart, "There is no God."
PSALM 53:1

What does it take to move from atheism to belief in God? A near-death experience, a loud voice from heaven, or a still quiet voice within saying, "There's more to life than what you see"?

For Dr Paul Brand, it was the intricacies of the human hand. As this skillful surgeon began to understand how marvelous the human hand is, he said this alone would be enough to make him believe in God.

A belief in God is not simply a theological or philosophical matter, not the bottom line of persuasion, nor the winning argument. It is the result of simple faith. The writer of Hebrews in the New Testament puts it, "And without faith it is impossible to please God, because anyone who comes to him must believe that he exists and that he rewards those who earnestly seek him" (Hebrews 11:6).

Thousands of men and women around the world, finding themselves torn between belief and unbelief, have cried out, "God, if you are there, please show me." Did the heavens open or did they experience a clap of thunder? Usually not. Did they find an answer? Always.

365 Guidelines for Daily Living

My Father's House

Now I am going to him who sent me.

JOHN 16:5

What makes a house a home? It's your family, the ones you love with all their faults and failures, your own flesh and blood. It's the love that is there because you belong to each other. As Dorothy from *The Wizard of Oz* claims, "Be it ever so humble, there's no place like home."

When I first began my ministry, my wife and I traveled extensively. In the lining of the old brown Samsonite suitcase that we used, we pinned the key to my father's house on South Madison so it would not get lost. Opening the suitcase, weary and tired, and seeing that key reminded me, "At the end of the trip, I'm going home." It gave me comfort to know that when I finally got there, I had the key to unlock the door.

Jesus said that He was the key that unlocked the door to his Father's home we call heaven. "I am the way and the truth and the life. No one comes to the Father except through me" (John 14:6). By the way, do you have such a key in your suitcase?

365 Guidelines for Daily Living

Overcoming Your Handicap

My grace is sufficient for you; for my power is
made perfect in weakness.

2 CORINTHIANS 12:9

What is the handicap that you live with? Paul said that he lived with a thorn in the flesh—perhaps a myopic condition that caused his eyes to water and run. Yet Paul said that through his weakness God's strength was more evident. When Paul asked God to remove his handicap, God replied, "My grace is sufficient for you; for my power is made perfect in weakness" (2 Corinthians 12:9).

God's strength is evident despite weakness. That means there can be beauty in life when a face is anything but beautiful. It means there can be strength in spite of physical weakness. There can be courage and integrity in spite of any physical condition. The strength that counts—and the one that changes the external —is the strength of character and integrity that begins from within.

When we face a handicap, there are two choices open to us. We can use the handicap as a crutch to fall back on, excusing our failures and shortcomings, or we can take it as a challenge and ask God to help us overcome our weakness.

Today Can Be the Best Day of Your Life

Believe and Achieve

Whatever you do, work at it with all your heart,
as working for the Lord, not for men.

COLOSSIANS 3:23

Defeatism never accomplished anything lasting or worthwhile. But optimism, born of faith, has accomplished tremendous feats. Surprising as it is to some people, optimism born of faith has its roots in God's Word, the Bible. Consider statements such as these: "For as he thinketh in his heart, so is he" (Proverbs 23:7 KJV). "Whatever you do, work at it with all your heart, as working for the Lord, not for men" (Colossians 3:23).

Men have been challenged with concepts or goals that others have said were impossible or unattainable. But they refused to believe them. With God's help they reached them.

There is a limit to what you can do naturally, but there is absolutely no limit to what can be accomplished in faith, through God's power.

Do not listen to the voice of pessimism, which says, "You are trapped—you cannot do it. You might as well quit, for it cannot be done." Quietly resolve in your heart, "With God's help, I'll do what He wants me to do," and you will discover that what your mind can conceive, with God's help, you can achieve.

Today Can Be the Best Day of Your Life

Why Not Make a Commitment?

If anyone would come after me, he must deny himself and take up his cross daily and follow me.

MATTHEW 16:24

How deep is your spiritual commitment? You've made the decision to receive Jesus Christ, but have you made a commitment to know Him, obey Him and serve Him?

When it comes to your commitment to Jesus Christ, God does not force you to enlist in His cause—He invites you. In Romans 12:1-2, Paul wrote, "I urge you brothers, in view of God's mercy, to offer your bodies as living sacrifices, holy and pleasing to God. . . . Do not conform any longer to the pattern of this world, but be transformed by the renewing of your mind."

The words "offer your bodies as living sacrifices" are active words. They are the same words used to describe pagans who offered sacrifices to heathen gods.

If you hesitate, there's a fundamental issue you need to settle: Is God good? If your answer is yes, you've eliminated your hesitation to trust Him and commit yourself to His care. Apart from commitment, there is no hope for anything enduring, including heaven itself.

Today Can Be the Best Day of Your Life

Who's on Trial—God or You?

When I am afraid, I will trust in You. In God, whose word I praise, in God I trust; I will not be afraid.

PSALM 56:3-4

Whenever tragedy strikes, it's easy to harden our hearts and cry out, "God, why did you let this happen?" Have you ever caught yourself calling God to account? Have you questioned the way He seemed to be working in your life?

If we could but see life from God's perspective, how different our attitudes would be. How much more quickly could we grasp the plan that lies just beyond our reach. How much more could we trust, realizing that His way is better than ours because He sees the end from the beginning.

Ultimately the answer lies in one word—*trust*. God loves us and we can entrust to Him our lives, hopes, even our futures. When difficulty knocks it's we who are on trial—not God. The more you know about the character of God, the easier it will be for you to say, "God knows best and I'll trust Him no matter what!"

Today Can Be Different

The Point of Prayer

In the day of my trouble I will call to you, for you will answer me.

PSALM 86:7

"To be a Christian without prayer," said Martin Luther, "is no more possible than to be alive without breathing." Prayer is the only way of becoming what God wants us to be. This is the reason why Jesus spent many hours in prayer.

Unquestionably, our needs bring us to a place of prayer. Confronted with danger, we look for God's help.

Difficult times always cause the hearts of men to turn to God in prayer. Nahum, the prophet, testifies, "The Lord is good, a stronghold in the day of trouble" (Nahum 1:7).

How long has it been since you've brought your burdens to God? Since you asked His forgiveness for your shortcomings? Because prayer is based on a relationship with God, be sure He is your Father, that you are His child. Be sure you're on good speaking terms with Him. "Ask, and you will receive," promised Christ, "that your joy may be made full" (John 16:24).

Today Can Be Different

April

I KNOW THAT MY REDEEMER LIVES,
AND THAT IN THE END HE
WILL STAND UPON THE EARTH.

JOB 19:25

Searching for God

*You will seek the LORD your God, and you will
find Him if you search for Him with all your
heart and all your soul.*

DEUTERONOMY 4:29 NASB

"The problem with you Christians," commented an
atheist, "is that you have monopolized all the
holidays. You have Christmas, Easter, Good Friday,
All Saints Day, and what-have-you. What we atheists
need is a holiday of our own."

A friend remembered Psalm 53:1—"The fool says in
his heart, 'There is no God.'" And so he countered with
a smile, "How about April 1?"

Nobody can fully prove the existence of God to anybody. But nobody can disprove it either. Writing the
first verse of the Bible, Moses began simply, "In the
beginning God . . ." (Genesis 1:1).

Where do you find God? In nature? Not really;
nature can be destructive when its storms sweep across
land and sea. In the human heart? That's risky; the
Holocaust and overflowing prisons dim the image of
God in man.

If you really want to find God, look for Him in the
person of His Son, Jesus Christ. "Anyone who has seen
me," Jesus told His followers, "has seen the Father"
(John 14:9).

Today Can Be Different

When You Become a Victim of Evil

And there was war in heaven. Michael and his angels fought against the dragon, and the dragon and his angels fought back.

REVELATION 12:7

After an arsonist burned down his church, Pastor Ted Cole picked his way through the still smoldering rubble and sat down at the piano. He began playing an old hymn written more than four centuries ago by a man who knew trouble well—Martin Luther. This particular hymn bears testimony to God's provision for every person who is assaulted by hostile forces: "A mighty fortress is our God, a bulwark never failing; our helper He amidst the flood of mortal ills prevailing."

Seeing the whole picture from God's perspective makes all the difference in the world. Proverbs 21:30 says, "There is no wisdom, no insight, no plan that can succeed against the LORD."

Until Christ returns, people with warped minds will burn down churches, assault innocent people, and mistreat others with no provocation. Driven by the hatred of Satan himself, they will slander and lie, but they can be overcome through the blood of Jesus and the power of our testimony.

Tomorrow Begins Today

When You Feel Beaten Up by Circumstances

The Lord is good. When trouble comes, he is the place to go! And he knows everyone who trusts in Him!

NAHUM 1:7 TLB

What do you do when you feel beaten up by the circumstances of life? Sit at home and feel sorry for yourself? If you have a relationship with the Father through His Son, remind yourself of the following truths:

GUIDELINE 1: You are God's child. When you feel beaten up by circumstances, remind yourself that feelings of worthlessness don't come from God.

GUIDELINE 2: God never promised to exempt you from trouble, but to be with you in times of trouble.

GUIDELINE 3: Nothing is forever. Instead of thinking of your situation as fatal, think of it as an opportunity to explore new areas of possibility and regroup.

GUIDELINE 4: Do your part. God does for us what we can't do ourselves. But if you lost your job, for example, He most probably won't motivate someone to call you and beg you to go to work for him.

It is the connection with your Father in heaven that keeps you from getting beaten up by the circumstances of life.

Tomorrow Begins Today

Quiet Your Heart

Be still, and know that I am God.

PSALM 46:10

*W*e're missing something today, something vital, something meaningful. It is the stillness that allows us to think, to listen, to ponder, and to plan.

God says, "Be still." That means shutting off your engine. Don't just turn down the volume. Shut it off. Put the kids to bed, go out to the backyard, and look at the stars. You'll be amazed at how difficult it is to find a quiet place. Even nature has its own kind of noise, though one that's restorative rather than numbing.

Yet being still isn't all that God wants us to learn. He says, "Be still, and know that I am God." The voice of God is a still one, and we hear His voice most clearly when we silence our hearts before Him.

You will never learn the benefits of stillness without reprogramming yourself. Try turning off your radio or TV for an evening. See how difficult it is—at least for most of us—to maintain an hour of silence.

There is strength in quiet and solitude. Isaiah 30 contains an interesting phrase: "In quietness and trust is your strength" (Isaiah 30:15). Yet Isaiah notes that the Israelites would not quiet their hearts before God. May we learn a lesson from their failure.

Tomorrow Can Be Beautiful

White-Water Rapids

We will not fear, though the . . . waters roar and foam and the mountains quake with their surging.

PSALM 46:2-3

I remember my first white-water rafting trip. I'd been around water ever since I was a little kid, so when they gave me a life jacket, I thought, "I don't need this thing, and besides, we were putting the raft into water that was placid and calm."

In a few minutes, the water started flowing more rapidly. After a few curves, I noticed the raft in front of us was wafting like a potato chip in the wind. "So that's what they call white water," I thought.

The helmsman yelled for us to paddle left, then right, then hard left. Then—whoosh! I suddenly found myself in the water, fighting for breath, trying to get my feet pointed downstream.

White-water rafting and life are similar in that you don't know where the rocks are or what's around the corner. When you get dunked and are gasping for breath, you want help and you want it now.

When life turns into a white-water experience, turn to Psalm 46. When God is your refuge, the intensity of the white waters isn't all that important.

Tomorrow Can Be Beautiful

The Importance of Now

I tell you the truth, whoever hears my word and believes him who sent me has eternal life and will not be condemned; he has crossed over from death to life.

JOHN 5:24

Four men were arguing about the best time to cut an ash stick. One man said that the best time was in the spring when the sap was rising. Another said, "No, summer is the best time, because then the wood is at its height." The third disagreed entirely. "The fall," he said, "is the best time, because the sap has matured and seasoned the wood." The fourth argued that winter was best because by then there was not any sap at all and the wood could be cut smoothly.

Finally, they decided to ask the expert. He listened to their arguments and then replied, "The best time to cut an ash stick, gentlemen, is when you see one, because it may not be there the next time you pass by."

God tells us that the time to do something about eternity is NOW—not tomorrow. What preparation have you made for the moment in your life when your watch becomes meaningless as time becomes eternity? No, not life insurance, or a will, or income for those you leave behind. I am thinking of preparation for eternity. Jesus called it eternal life.

Tomorrow Can Be Beautiful

The God Factor in Stress Management

Don't fret or worry. Instead of worrying, pray.
Let petitions and praises shape your worries into
prayers, letting God know your concerns.

PHILIPPIANS 4:6 TM

*T*rusting God doesn't eliminate the problem you have with your difficult boss, or erase the stress factors in your life. But when you take what the New Testament says and apply it to your life, it makes a big difference.

For example, read Matthew 6 and notice what Jesus says about how God cares for the birds of the air. Then ask yourself the question, "Am I not much more valuable than they?"

Memorize Philippians 4:6, which says in *The Living Bible*, "Don't worry about anything; instead, pray about everything; tell God your needs and don't forget to thank Him for His answers."

Knowing that God is your heavenly Father helps you put life in perspective. Fifty years from now, the cares of today won't matter. But your relationship with God will count even when the stars have burned themselves out and become cinders. Because God loves you and is in control of your life, a lot of what causes stress isn't worth the worry.

Tomorrow Can Be Beautiful

Loving in Slices

Accept one another, then, just as Christ accepted you, in order to bring praise to God.

ROMANS 15:7

can't love people in slices," says King Arthur in *Camelot*, "I take the good with the bad." Maybe that's why King Arthur presided successfully over a vast array of knights—and we preside over relationships gone bad.

Can we love people in slices, choosing what we like, rejecting what we dislike? Come to think of it, nobody, myself included, is completely lovable. In every person there is a diversity of attitudes, habits, and mannerisms—some wonderful, and some quite annoying.

Can we just choose those parts in the person that make us feel good? Is this love?

Love is more than a warm feeling; it is a commitment to care, a decision of the heart, which has nothing to do with the temperature of our feelings.

What causes us to love in slices is plain selfishness. We do not want the pain and sacrifice involved in loving the whole person. The result is loneliness and estrangement.

Taking the good with the bad is the only way to go.

365 Guidelines for Daily Living

Rediscovering the Amazing Grace of God

But Noah found grace in the eyes of the Lord.
GENESIS 6:8 KJV

Is grace one of those truths lost by a "me generation" in search of instant fulfillment and happiness?

The word in the Bible translated *grace* is one used of kings or emperors who treated their subjects with undeserved kindness or blessing. Does the same concept apply to the way in which the Creator, the Lord of the universe, treats us, His created beings? Yes! In simple terms, grace means an unmerited, undeserved favor. A generation ago, C. I. Scofield in the notes of the reference Bible that bears his name, said, "Grace is the kindness and love of God our Savior toward man . . ." (see John 1:12).

Grace has to do with what God has done for us. Mercy is not getting what we deserve, while grace is getting what we don't deserve. A child caught taking cookies from a cookie jar may not receive a spanking —that's mercy. But the gift of more cookies than the child could eat in a lifetime is what grace is about.

A simple but good definition of grace is an acrostic based on the letters

G–R–A–C–E: "God's Riches At Christ's Expense."

Today Can Be the Best Day of Your Life

Another Day

Therefore do not worry about tomorrow, for tomorrow will worry about itself. Each day has enough trouble of its own.

MATTHEW 6:34

This isn't just another day. This is today, the most important day of your life. It's the only day that you can do something about.

Just for today, strive to do God's will, remembering that the failures of yesterday are behind you. When you wake in the morning, learn to say, "God, please walk with me today. Help me to live today as though it were the last day of my life."

Live today as though you would meet your Maker at the end of the day. Paul wrote," Today is the day of salvation" (1 Corinthians 6:2). If you have no peace in your heart, reach out to the loving Savior, and invite Him to come into your life and give you the assurance that if you met God at the end of the day, you would not be ashamed to call Him Father. It has been said that life is a series of todays that so quickly turn into yesterdays to which some of us spend our time regretfully looking backward. Still others, through worry or procrastination, are always waiting for tomorrow. Focus on today!

Today Can Be the Best Day of Your Life

Just a Smile, Please

A happy heart makes the face cheerful, but heartache crushes the spirit.

PROVERBS 15:13

I've seen pictures of Jesus—at least as artists and sculptors have imagined Him—in the art galleries of the world. Most are sober while some reflect tenderness, compassion, and great love. But I cannot recall ever seeing a picture of Jesus smiling. Why is that?

It's certain that Jesus smiled. Does the text tell us that? No, but the context does. Who could hold a little child and not smile? Jesus no doubt laughed with His disciples and expressed the joy of His life.

People rarely smile when they are fearful, uptight, and full of stress. A genuine smile is an expression of an overflowing heart of love. Paul tells us that the fruit of the indwelling Spirit of God includes love, joy, and peace (Galatians 5:22–23). We can smile because we know that God is in charge of the world and our lives.

There are times when it is difficult to smile. But it is never impossible. Is there anyone in your life who makes it hard for you to smile? That person is God's challenge to you. Go on, relax and give that person a smile. You just might discover something really worth smiling about.

Tomorrow Begins Today

Suffering and the Promises of God

All kinds of trials . . . have come so that your faith . . . may be proved genuine and may result in praise, glory and honor when Jesus Christ is revealed.

1 PETER 1:6-7

There is a common perception today that faith in Jesus Christ will exempt you from the trials and hardships of life, especially with regard to health, happiness, and prosperity. Yet when people buy this idea and discover later that their prayers do not always turn back the hostility of the world, they are disappointed.

In his first letter, Peter says the believer's response should not be hostility but rather joyfulness because the Spirit of glory and of Christ rests in him. Here are some principles that you can remember:

1 Times of difficulty are accompanied by a promise of His presence. In Matthew 28:20, Jesus promised, "I am with you always . . . ."

2 Our trials also come with the promise of His protection (1 Peter 1:5).

3 There is also the promise of His cleansing. Although we would rather avoid difficult times, good always comes out of them. Peter compared our faith to gold which is put in the furnace to be refined.

Today Can Be the Best Day of Your Life

Is There an End to the Storm?

Give thanks to the LORD Almighty, for the LORD is good; his love endures forever.

JEREMIAH 33:11

Tough times pass, but tough people—those who are focused on what God says about our lives—endure. Such a man was the prophet Jeremiah. His beloved country, Israel, was about to be overthrown by Babylon. Jeremiah had to announce this prophecy, a message that was denounced as "unpatriotic and traitorous."

Yet Jeremiah looked beyond the external events and heard the voice of God. Yes, Israel would go into captivity for seventy years. But God promised restoration. "'For I know the plans I have for you,' declares the LORD, 'plans to prosper you and not to harm you, plans to give you hope and a future'" (Jeremiah 29:11).

So certain was Jeremiah that God would keep His word, that he bought a piece of property that lay in default, burying the title deed in a jar so that when the troubles had passed, he could come back and claim the property (see Jeremiah 32).

Your life may seem like a catastrophe, but the story is not yet finished. You can lean on God and say, "I trust You Lord, so please walk with me today."

365 Guidelines for Daily Living

Choices or Sins?

But there is forgiveness with thee, that thou
mayest be feared.

PSALM 130:4 KJV

"I have sinned" is a phrase seldom used today in accounting for our misdeeds. The first use of that phrase recorded in the Bible was by Pharaoh, during the plague of locusts in Egypt (Exodus 10:16). The next person was Balaam, a sort of New Age guru before his time, whose donkey had more sense than he did (Numbers 22:34). In the New Testament, both Judas Iscariot (Matthew 27:4) and the prodigal son (Luke 15:21) confessed, "I have sinned."

It may be difficult to acknowledge your personal responsibility for wrongdoing (which the Bible calls sin), but confession opens the door to forgiveness and life. God forgives sin, but the stupidity of refusing to acknowledge your sin is unforgivable.

Forgiveness is the solution to our human failure, but until we are forthright and honest enough to admit we have sinned, we continue to walk in darkness.

Tomorrow Begins Today

Understanding the Heart of God

I will give them a heart to know me, that I am the LORD. They will be my people, and I will be their God.

JEREMIAH 24:7

There are barriers that impair our knowledge of God's heart. The first is our sinful nature. We cannot understand the heart of God until we first understand that man's heart has been darkened by sin and rebellion against God.

The second barrier is our self-centeredness. God said, "You will seek me and find me when you seek me with all your heart" (Jeremiah 29:13). We must focus upon Him, strive to see life from His perspective, and understand how differently He views our lives and problems.

The third barrier is our ignorance of the nature and character of God. The prophet Hosea wrote, "My people are destroyed from lack of knowledge" (Hosea 4:6). His lament is far more descriptive of our generation than any one in recent years.

Can we really know the heart of God? Indeed we can. Knowing the heart of God brings all of life into focus, and the path of discovery is the way of life itself.

Today Can Be the Best Day of Your Life

We Do Not Lose Heart

So we fix our eyes not on what is seen, but on what is unseen. For what is seen is temporary, but what is unseen is eternal.

2 CORINTHIANS 4:18

Seldom does a writer open his heart and reveal his soul, yet there are times when individuals open the window shades and let you see within.

I think of the fourth chapter of 2 Corinthians, which some have called the "heart of Paul." Here Paul describes the difficult side of his work. Twice he says, "therefore . . . we do not lose heart" (2 Corinthians 4:1,16). The word Paul used is found three times in the New Testament, including in his letter to the Ephesians, where it is translated "to be discouraged."

Paul had learned something that we need to learn today, something that's often missing in our lives. He learned that the only way to survive the battles of life is a fresh encounter with God's mercy and help.

He also learned to stay focused on what really mattered—"not on what is seen but on what is unseen" (2 Corinthians 4:18). The love of a wife, the camaraderie of a friend, the value of your integrity, and your faith in God are all commodities that are unseen. Make these the fabric of what counts for eternity.

Today Can Be the Best Day of Your Life

Conscience

How much more will the blood of Christ, who
through the eternal Spirit offered Himself
without blemish to God, cleanse your conscience
from dead works to serve the living God?

HEBREWS 9:14 NASB

A woman once left a set of diamond rings on a ledge in a restroom. When she remembered this minutes later, she frantically returned to find them, but her rings were gone. Fifteen years later, however, she again held them in her hands. They arrived by airmail with a note that read, "May God forgive."

What prompts people to return items after so long? The answer lies in a single word, "conscience." It is God's supreme court in your heart, passing moral and spiritual judgment based on the knowledge you possess.

Psychiatrists have attempted to deny the effects of conscience. They may convince someone to try to still the voice of conscience, but they cannot remove the guilt of conscience. Christ alone can do that.

The Savior is loving and compassionate. To Him you can pour out the deepest feelings of your heart and find a refuge. The book of Hebrews exhorts, "Let us draw near [to God] with a sincere heart in full assurance of faith, having our hearts sprinkled clean from an evil conscience" (10:22 NASB).

Today Can Be Different

The Will of God

So then do not be foolish, but understand what the will of the Lord is.

EPHESIANS 5:17 NASB

In recent years, science has done much to explain the order and accuracy of a universe that has been in operation for untold centuries. But almost 3,500 years ago, Moses explained the order in nature: "In the beginning, God created the heavens and the earth" (Genesis 1:1). But the Bible doesn't stop there; it says that God not only had a plan for our universe, He has a plan for our lives. Paul said we are to demonstrate what is the good, perfect, and acceptable will of God (see Romans 12:1–2).

Often we are willing to trust God for guidance involving our big life decisions, like who we will marry and what kind of job we will have, and totally ignore His will concerning the little decisions that eventually set the stage for the bigger ones. Actually, life is made up of the little decisions—the shredded wheat and peanut butter decisions of everyday living. Consider the space shuttle to the moon—it will never get to its destination unless all the little parts function properly. Trust God day by day to reveal the good and acceptable and perfect will for your life.

Today Can Be Different

Praying for Your Pastor

*Pray also for me, that whenever I open my mouth,
words may be given me so that I will fearlessly
make known the mystery of the gospel.*

EPHESIANS 6:19-20

When J. Wilbur Chapman was a young pastor,
several people came to him and said, "Mr. Chapman, we have had other pastors in this church who were
better preachers than you are, and in time they failed.
We think you will probably fail, too. However, we are
going to pray for you." And pray they did—earnestly,
fervently—that God would bless the life and ministry
of this young man. What happened to Chapman? He
became a powerful evangelist through whom thousands
of people came to a saving knowledge of Jesus Christ.

Wherever you find men and women who serve God,
whether it is a lonely patriarch with his arms outstretched towards the army of Israel, or a country
preacher or missionary laboring in a forgotten place,
you will find people who pray.

Don't forget to pray for your pastor and others you
know who are in ministry. It can make all the difference
between their being a failure and a success.

365 Guidelines for Daily Living

Miniaturization

Can you bind the beautiful Pleiades? Can you loose the cords of Orion?

JOB 38:31

Today, scientists are able to compress more and more information in a given space as the result of the growth of computer technology. The world's largest library, for example, can be reduced to microfilm stored in a standard, four-drawer filing cabinet—the kind you find in most offices.

Yet with all these advances, there are still some things that cannot be shrunk: loneliness in the hearts of men and women, the sorrow that a parent experiences at the loss of a child, or the emptiness of a life lived without purpose or meaning.

Kids who search for identity by painting graffiti on the walls are not looking for "information." Nor does "information" satisfy a little child's craving to be held and loved. The emptiness of the human heart will never be shrunk by scientific technology, for the human heart was meant to store love—God's love and the love of family, friends, and people who care. Technology is fine, but it is no substitute for a loving heart.

Greater than the universe itself, God alone can fill the inner space of the human heart.

365 Guidelines for Daily Living

The Solution to a Troubled Life

He who conceals his sins does not prosper,
but whoever confesses and renounces them
finds mercy.

PROVERBS 28:13

King David must have felt that his morality was a private matter. Running the kingdom was one thing; what he did in private was something else. Yet it all exploded in his face when he had an affair with Bathsheba and tried to hide it (2 Samuel 11–12). One day the prophet Nathan told David the story of a wealthy man who stole a lamb from a poor man. He asked David what should be done to such a man. David was outraged at the rich man's wrongdoing. But Nathan turned to David and said, "You are that man!"

Just as it was for David, you can be sure your sin will find you out. The solution? First—confess. Coming clean and admitting your failure is the first step. Second—forsake your wrongdoing, and go a different direction. It's the only lasting solution.

Today Can Be the Best Day of Your Life

Long-Suffering

*Remember me . . . and avenge me on my
persecutors. You are long-suffering—do not take
me away; think of how I suffer reproach for
your sake.*

JEREMIAH 15:15

ave you ever faced a difficult situation when your
heart cried out, "God, where are You? Why don't
You do something?" Habakkuk voiced the same plea
when he saw the Babylonians punishing Israel. He cried,
"How long, O Lord, must I call for help, but you do not
listen?" (Habakkuk 1:2)

The Bible speaks of long-suffering mostly in reference to God's gracious patience with His people. But
God is not weak or unable to step into a situation and
correct in immediately. God will call all into account
someday. Just because God is being gracious and
patient with you, don't think for a moment that He
ignores wrongdoing forever. Paul said that we should
count God's long-suffering as salvation (2 Peter 3:15)

Thank God that He is long-suffering, but realize that
He is also just. God is God and He is in control, no
matter how insane the world may seem.

Tomorrow Can Be Beautiful

The Voice of the Lord

Give ear and hear my voice, listen and hear my words.

ISAIAH 28:23 NASB

How do we recognize the voice of God, as opposed to the voice of Satan or something else? It through His word, the Bible, that we most often hear God's voice today.

The words of Jesus are recorded in Revelation 3:20 (NASB), as He says, "Behold, I stand at the door and knock; if anyone hears My voice and opens the door, I will come in to him and will dine with him, and he with Me." I would not presume to tell you that God cannot speak directly to your heart. But I can tell you that He will never speak anything to your heart that contradicts what He has said in His Word.

God is trying to tell us more than we have heard. His voice is drowned out by a thousand other voices that clamor for our attention. Want to hear His voice more clearly? Take time to read His letters to you in the Bible and meditate on what you have learned. Listen to His voice in prayer. The voice of God is saying, "Here's the path to real heaven. Here's the way to live."

Today Can Be the Best Day of Your Life

Accepting Change

Every good and perfect gift is from above, coming down from the Father of the heavenly lights, who does not change like shifting shadows.

JAMES 1:17

Why is it so difficult to accept change—whether related to our country, job, or family—when it is certain that we who object to change are changing at the same time we object to the changes around us?

Accepting change is never easy. For instance, consider the elderly gentleman whose eyesight has deteriorated to the point where he can no longer drive. Yet he still holds on to his driver's license and renews it every year, even though he knows that if he drives he will be a danger to everyone, including himself.

Accepting what we really are is part of maturity. The inevitability of change can be accepted as gracefully as the coming of the spring flowers after winter, or it can be as difficult as a winter blizzard or a typhoon that sweeps across the South China Sea.

Whether you fight change or accommodate it gracefully depends largely on your perception of what lies ahead. For the child of God, moving towards heaven only sharpens the focus on eternity. This gives light to negotiate the changes gracefully. Your faith can make the difference.

Today Can Be the Best Day of Your Life

The Influence of a Life

These commandments that I give you today are
to be upon your hearts. Impress them on your
children. Talk about them when you sit at home
and when you walk along the road, when you lie
down and when you get up.

DEUTERONOMY 6:6–7

It's my life—let me live it like I want to." If you have
never said it, you have probably thought it, for
nearly everyone at times feels that he must make his
own decisions. Few of us realize, however, the far-
reaching effects of the decisions we make.

I once asked a pastor if his father was a Christian.
He replied, "Yes, and a great many before him." It happened like this: Nearly a hundred years ago, two
brothers went to a meeting, thinking it would be great
fun to break it up. But as they listened to the speaker,
their interest was captured. Finally, when the speaker
invited those present to make a commitment to Christ,
one of the brothers did so. The other brother turned in
disgust and left.

Since then, some 170 have followed in the steps of
the brother who had chosen Christ. But, on the side
of the other brother, not one person had become a
Christian. The influence of a life is far greater than we
often realize.

Today Can Be Different

Accidents or Incidents?

And we know that in all things God works for the good of those who love him, who have been called according to his purpose.

ROMANS 8:28

When things go wrong in life, do we assume that what happened is an accident? Or can we accept the fact that there are no accidents, only incidents for God's children—incidents that demonstrate human weakness and show how God's grace is sufficient no matter what the situation is?

Though we may not fully understand how or why, the promise that Paul made to the believers in Rome is yet valid. "And we know," he wrote, "that in all things God works for the good of those who love him, who have been called according to his purpose."

God is in control. There are no accidents for the child of God, only incidents that bring us into confrontation with our humanness and God's sovereign grace.

365 Guidelines for Daily Living

Molecules and Spiritual Laws

He is before all things, and in Him all things hold together.

COLOSSIANS 1:17 NASB

Almost unbelievable, yet true in our seeing-is-believing world, is the fact that no one has ever seen a molecule with the naked eye. In fact, scientists have not yet stopped a molecule on film, even with today's fast cameras under high-powered microscopes.

A molecule is the smallest bit of substance that can exist and still keep the properties of the whole. If you take a molecule of sugar and divide it, the particles will lose the properties of sugar.

Though a scientist cannot give any visible proof of molecules, he knows they exist because he sees the evidence of their invisible reality. The same is true of the existence of God: Though His existence cannot be proved, neither can the evidence of His existence be denied. God is the power that holds all of Creation together, that creation which He spoke into existence in the beginning by His words (see Genesis 1:1–2:2).

When it comes both to God and to molecules, the same principle is true: Faith rooted in evidence points to their existence.

Today Can Be Different

In Times of Trouble

And call upon me in the day of trouble: I will
deliver thee, and thou shalt glorify me.

PSALM 50:15 KJV

God—unlike some earthly parents—treats all His children the same way. If God moves especially quick to help some, it is for the child whose faith is weak, the widow who has no one to defend her, the person struggling with feelings of inadequacy and failure.

The bottom line is, "Are you willing to trust God?" Let's say you have reached the limits of your faith. Are you willing to pray, "Lord, I want to believe; help me overcome my unbelief"?

People who walk with God through the fire discover what Liddie Edmonds, who wrote the words of my favorite hymn, experienced:

> *My faith has found a resting place,*
> *Not in device or creed;*
> *I trust the ever living One.*
> *His wounds for me shall plead.*
> *I need no other argument,*
> *I need no other plea;*
> *It is enough that Jesus died,*
> *And that He died for me.*

365 Guidelines for Daily Living

What a Way to Go

I have fought the good fight, I have finished the race, I have kept the faith. Now there is in store for me the crown of righteousness, which the Lord, the righteous Judge, will award to me on that day.

2 TIMOTHY 4:7-8

Some people live in denial of their humanity. Never will they mention the thought of death, dying, or eternity. Why? Because they are paralyzed with fear.

If we believe that matters of life and death are important to our heavenly Father—and part of the cycle of life—there's no reason not to talk about them.

If I were going to Buckingham Palace for an audience with the queen, I'd talk about it—what to wear, what to say, and how to conduct myself. Should we be less concerned about our entrance into the presence of the King of Kings and Lord of Lords?

If you believe the Bible, you know that God has a purpose and will for every person. When your life is purpose-driven, you can say with Paul, "I have fought the good fight, I have finished the race, I have kept the faith" (2 Timothy 4:7).

"Dost thou love life?" asked Benjamin Franklin, "Then use time wisely, for that's the stuff that life is made of."

Tomorrow Can Be Beautiful

The Divine "A"

Why are thou cast down, O my soul? and why art thou disquieted in me? hope thou in God: for I shall yet praise him for the help of his countenance.

PSALM 42:5 KJV

One day Arturo Toscanini read this brief note from a fan in a small town in Wyoming: "Dear Sir: I'm a lonely sheepherder, and the only company I have is my violin and a small battery radio. I'm afraid that soon my batteries will be dead and I won't be able to hear you any more. Then all I'll have for company is my old fiddle. It is so badly out of tune that I cannot play it until I get it back in pitch. Would you be so kind as to sound the note of 'A' this Sunday night on your broadcast? Sincerely . . ." and he signed his name.

This touched a responsive chord in Toscanini's heart. That Sunday night the program announcer said, "Now, for our dear friend with the out-of-tune violin, here's the note of 'A.'" That note sounded throughout New York City, and miles away, the lonely sheepherder tuned the violin to pitch.

Do you see a parallel to what happened 2,000 years ago when Christ came to our broken world? If the story reminds you of your life, why not let God bring you back into pitch with life?

365 Guidelines for Daily Living

May

HE HAS SHOWN KINDNESS
BY GIVING YOU RAIN FROM HEAVEN
AND CROPS IN THEIR SEASONS;
HE PROVIDES YOU WITH PLENTY
OF FOOD AND FILLS YOUR HEART
WITH JOY.

ACTS 14:17

The Right to be Happy

And having food and raiment let us be therewith content.

1 TIMOTHY 6:8 KJV

*R*obert Louis Stevenson said, "The world is so full of a number of things, I'm sure we should all be as happy as kings." Yet, we're not all that happy. Why?

There is something far more important than happiness: Joy. Happiness is the world's substitute for true joy. What's the difference?

Happiness depends on circumstances; joy transcends your circumstances. (You can be joyful even when you are not happy.)

Happiness involves your environment—your home, money, friends, health. But joy comes from within.

Happiness is temporary; joy abides and remains even when beauty fades.

Happiness has little to do with God; joy has everything to do with Him.

Happiness is material; joy is spiritual.

Happiness involves your life here and now; joy encompasses time and eternity.

When you find God, you discover joy; and when you joyfully do God's will, you'll stumble over happiness. You can never be happier than being where God wants you to be—no matter where it is.

Tomorrow Begins Today

If You Only Knew

*Just as man is destined to die once, and after that
to face judgment, so Christ was sacrificed once to
take away the sins of many people.*

HEBREWS 9:27

If you knew you had only sixty days to live, what would you do? That was the question I asked at a staff meeting one Monday morning. For a few seconds it was very quiet and sober. "Well, for one thing," said one man in jest, "I'd stop paying my bills!"

Long ago, Moses sat and wrote down, "The length of our days is seventy years—or eighty . . . . Yet their span is but trouble and sorrow, for they quickly pass and we fly away." Then he cried from the heart, "Teach us to number each of our days aright, that we may gain a heart of wisdom" (see Psalm 90).

If you only had sixty days to live, would you ask forgiveness from someone you've hurt? Clear your conscience by returning what you took years ago? Tell your spouse, your children, and your parents how much you love them?

I know one thing for sure. A lot of people would make peace with God if they knew their time was running out. Wise is the person who doesn't leave things until the last sixty days of his life.

Tomorrow Can Be Beautiful

Would Jesus Bloody His Knuckles?

I can do everything through him who gives me strength.

PHILIPPIANS 4:13

A popular pastime these days is searching for statements in the Bible to support our "God wants us to win" mentality. In simple terms, we want Jesus on our team, energizing us, enabling us to succeed.

When Paul talked about doing all things through God's strength, he was talking about persevering through difficulty—facing hunger, enduring derision, and surviving persecution, not sacking the quarterback or winning a football game. Every competitor does not win, but every person facing difficulty—the negative side of the ledger of life—can find God's power to cope, to endure, to survive the attacks of his enemies. Paul emphasizes that no matter what your circumstances are—good or bad—you can learn to be content and you can find God's help to overcome adversity.

Whether or not you "win the game," you will have won the battle of surviving difficulty in God's strength.

Tomorrow Can Be Beautiful

The Ragged Edge of Reality

For in the day of trouble he will keep me safe in his dwelling; he will hide me in the shelter of his tabernacle and set me high upon a rock.

PSALM 27:5

Joe Stowell calls it "the ragged edge of reality." This is the realization that your life is out of control, and you don't know what to do about it.

The ragged edge of reality can be painfully devastating. I probably don't have to describe it further. You know how it is when you've been there. But then, sometimes God allows us to face the ragged edge of reality so we'll stop playing games with Him, and get desperate enough to let Him help us.

Self-reliance may be an admirable trait in our society, but during desperate times, there are things that only God can do. The psalmist says, "For in the day of trouble he will keep me safe in his dwelling; he will hide me in the shelter of his tabernacle and set me high upon a rock."

Tomorrow Can Be Beautiful

Rewrite the Success Script of Your Life

And I saw that all labor and all achievement spring from man's envy of his neighbor. This too is meaningless, a chasing after the wind.

ECCLESIASTES 4:4

In most cases, we fail to find the happiness we want in life because our definition of success has only two dimensions: ourselves and our goals. True success, however, is three dimensional. God, and His purpose for our lives, must be included in any definition of success.

Was Jesus' life a success? He made statements such as, "I must be about my Father's business" (Luke 2:49 *KJV*), and "My food . . . is to do the will of him who sent me and to finish his work" (John 4:34). His agenda included a third dimension that gave Him a purpose beyond accomplishing certain objectives in life. Should we not have the same perspective?

The secret of success—real success—doesn't come through better management principles. It's relational. It has to include your family, your God, and yourself.

Friend, it may well be time to rewrite the script for your life. Focus on what God says about your roles in life and your purpose for each role. You may be far more successful than you've ever realized.

Tomorrow Can Be Beautiful

The Healing Power of Hope (1)

We, who were the first to hope in Christ, might be for the praise of his glory.

EPHESIANS 1:12

Many of us today are gripped with a quiet despair, uncertain of the future, wondering if there is hope for our generation. Science and technology have united to produce the greatest arsenal of weapons the world has ever known. Add to this the problems of food shortages, the energy crisis, and many other difficulties.

Where shall we look for hope? Shall we look in Moscow, Peking, Geneva, Bonn, or Washington? Little hope ebbs from the capitals of the world, but there is hope in a world considered hopeless by many.

The Bible says there is no hope in the heart of man apart from the hope that comes through faith in God. Faith becomes the doorway that provides hope for the future, and that makes our lives worth living now.

Today Can Be the Best Day of Your Life

The Healing Power of Hope (2)

But for you who revere my name, the sun of righteousness will rise with healing in its wings.

MALACHI 4:2

"Hope," said Thales, the Greek philosopher, "is the most universal thing in the world, for hope stays with those who have nothing else."

Many people are in despair because they have ruled out the very grounds of hope itself, which is God. In contrast, the believer's hope centers in Jesus Christ, who gave us the hope of eternal life and the assurance that there is more to life than the weariness of earning enough to keep ourselves from starving.

Hope is part of the armor of the soul, which is put there by God, and is vitally linked to the belief that He really controls and governs our eternal destiny. The Apostle Paul saw hope as a spiritual quality of the soul, based on the assurance that God exists above and beyond anything that man can do to the life of another man. Our destiny is really in God's hands!

Today Can Be the Best Day of Your Life

God Loves You "As Is"

And to know the love of Christ which surpasses knowledge.

EPHESIANS 3:19 NASB

People come in all shapes, sizes—and personalities! There are some who have carefully labeled individuals as choleric, sanguine, melancholic, and phlegmatic. But most of us don't fit neatly into one little box because our feelings and moods shift. At times we are confident and exuberant, fully in control, afraid of nothing; other times we are cautious, hesitant, fearful, and frustrated.

One of the most comforting truths of the Bible is that God knows and loves us just as we are. With Him we do not have to play games, pretending to be confident and "on top of things" when we're really down and fearful of what may happen.

No one else is a carbon copy of you. Just as no two snowflakes are the same no one else in all the world is exactly like you. Whether you're a vibrant extrovert or a shy introvert, you're one of a kind! God made you just as you are and His love for you is unchanging and unqualified.

Today Can Be Different

Four Laws of Answered Prayer

If you abide in Me, and My words abide in you, you will ask what you desire, and it shall be done for you.

JOHN 15:7 NKJV

Just as God has set into motion physical laws to govern the workings of our universe, so has He set "laws" in the spiritual realm regarding prayer.

LAW 1: *The law of relationship.* "If you abide in Me, and My words abide in you, you will ask what you desire, and it shall be done for you."

LAW 2: *The law of authority.* Jesus said, "And whatever you ask in My name, that I will do, that the Father may be glorified in the Son" (John 14:13 NKJV).

LAW 3: *The law of divine will.* "Now this is the confidence that we have in Him, that if we ask anything according to His will, He hears us" (1 John 5:14 NKJV).

LAW 4: *The law of faith.* Jesus said, "Assuredly, I say to you, if you have faith and do not doubt, you will not only do what was done to the fig tree, but also if you say to this mountain, 'Be removed and be cast into the sea,' it will be done" (Matthew 21:21 NKJV).

365 Guidelines for Daily Living

Others are Guilty, Not Me!

All of us like sheep have gone astray, each of us has turned to his own way; but the LORD has caused the iniquity of us all to fall on Him.

ISAIAH 53:6 NASB

When we see our neighbor do something wrong, we say his is a willful act of wrongdoing, but when we happen to do the same thing, we say it's just an "innocent mistake." Long ago Solomon recognized this flaw of man and said, "All the ways of a man are pure in his own eyes" (Proverbs 16:2 NKJV).

When a person knows right from wrong and rejects the right, he has no worthwhile alternative left. The person who lives according to what is right can look back and say, "I've done right!" whether it was recognized by others or not.

Two things are necessary: wisdom and integrity. Both play an important part in achieving success from God's perspective.

Today Can Be Different

Strength of the Mountain Mover

Have faith in God . . . if anyone says to this mountain, "Go, throw yourself into the sea," and does not doubt in his heart . . . it will be done for him.

MARK 11:22–23

*W*hen circumstances fog my goals and I'm thinking that my problem is too difficult for me, I turn to biblical truths that help hold me steady.

In Mark 11:22–23, Jesus was using a figure of speech. He was saying that God can do the impossible—move the mountain of doubt, fear, suffering, or an otherwise impossible situation. Jesus says that my response to His greatness is believing that He can do what I cannot do. The Bible calls this faith.

If you are climbing a mountain and the weather turns stormy, and you can't see your way to the top, waiting is hard. But there is spiritual discipline in learning to wait, for then we sense something of the awesome strength of God. It isn't the size of the mountain but the strength of the Mountain Mover that really counts.

Today Can Be Beautiful

Unwelcome Surprises

But he said to me, "My grace is sufficient for you, for my power is made perfect in weakness.

2 CORINTHIANS 12:9

The loss of a job, the death of a loved one, a financial disaster, or a storm that damages your town—how do you handle the unwelcome surprises of life? Psychologists call it "coping." Some think of it as "rolling with the punches." Others say with resignation, "That's life!" But when tragedies come our way, we respond in either one of two ways: We either fight them and become bitter, or we reach out for the grace of God and become better through what we have endured.

The Apostle Paul faced many unwelcome surprises, things he didn't deserve and certainly didn't ask for. But he wrote, "When I am weak," said Paul, "then I am strong" (2 Corinthians 12:10). When unwelcome surprises confront you, learn about grace, God's grace, and you will also find strength to cope. Poverty of spirit comes when we have depleted our resources, when our charm, looks, money, and connections are no longer enough to get us out of our jam. That's when we know we need God.

Tomorrow Begins Today

Circumstances

Even though I walk through the valley of the shadow of death, I will fear no evil, for you are with me.

PSALM 23:4

Two prospectors went to a desert in search of gold. They carefully noted every landmark, because to be lost could mean certain death. One night a great storm drove them into a cave. As they watched the storm sweep through the terrain, one of the prospectors cried in panic, "All the landmarks are swept away, and we are lost!" But the other man calmly said, "Wait! Soon the storm clouds will be gone, and we will see the sky." Sure enough, the clouds rolled back, and when the two prospectors saw the stars, they found their bearings yet again.

Two things give me peace amidst the storms of life. One is by looking at the stars, where I realize that the God who placed them above, eons of years ago, is the same today. Two is by remembering the ruins of ancient civilizations, where I realize that the problems confronting me today, like the civilizations of past, will not be with me forever.

When we look upward, God gives us our bearing in life's chaotic circumstances. He speaks to our hearts today amidst the thunder and roar of life.

Today Can Be the Best Day of Your Life

Jesus, the CEO

For the Son of Man came to seek and to save what was lost.

LUKE 19:10

A book whose title caught my attention is *Jesus, CEO*. It tries to identify good management principles in Jesus' life, but honestly, thinking of Jesus as a Chief Executive Officer doesn't sit well with me.

From the beginning Jesus made it clear that His kingdom was not of this world. He stated His mission clearly when he said, "For the Son of Man came to seek and to save what was lost" (Luke 19:10). His mission was to change the world, not to provide corporate leadership to the band of disciples who would eventually found His Church.

It's true that getting Christ out of the musty cathedral into the workplace is something we need to do. Following His instruction would change the way business is done by first changing the lives of those who do the business. It would bring fairness and honesty to the bargaining table. It would change the lot of the working man in ways that labor unions have never been able to accomplish.

But let's get it straight: Jesus was the only begotten Son of God, not the CEO of the early Church. There is a difference.

365 Guidelines for Daily Living

How Would You Like to be Remembered?

I will remember the deeds of the LORD . . . I will meditate on all your works and consider all of your mighty deeds.

PSALM 77:11-12

How would you like to be remembered when you die? In the Old Testament book of Chronicles are fascinating stories of famous and powerful people. Some went to their deaths in disgrace and some in fame and glory. Their life stories finish with a one-line summary. For example, King Jehoram was arrogant and ill-liked. He died at age 32 of an incurable disease. The chapter of his life closes with these words: "He passed away, to no one's regret, and was buried in the City of David, but not in the tombs of the kings" (2 Chronicles 21:20).

What a contrast to another king, Josiah, who lived a few generations later. Of him, it is written, "He was buried in the tombs of his fathers, and all Judah and Jerusalem mourned for him" (2 Chronicles 35:24).

If, for some reason, God draws a line at the end of your life tonight, how would you be remembered? No one knows when we should prepare the epitaph for our final resting place. Yet we are remembered both for what we are and what we do.

Today Can Be the Best Day of Your Life

If the Good Lord's Willing

The LORD is good, a refuge in times of trouble.
He cares for those who trust in him.

NAHUM 1:7

There's a line from a barbershop quartet song that goes, "If the Lord be willing, and the creek don't rise."

When the creek rises, and you face tragedy, the circumstances either drive you to God, or drive you away from Him. When you turn to Him, you find solace and strength, the kind that David discovered in the valley of the shadow of death (Psalm 23:4). When you turn away from God, you deprive yourself of the only real source of help there is. I've never quite understood why God gets blamed for the consequences of living in a human world.

It's okay to tell God how you feel, how crushed you are, and how much you wish something hadn't happened. The prophet Habakkuk certainly questioned God when He seemed to be standing aloof and silent when disaster struck. But God finally answered him. So listen for the answer, and you will learn that God is not silent in times of trouble. He's very much there, speaking to us about the brevity of life and the importance of including Him in our lives. Sometimes through sorrow, His quiet voice comes through the loudest.

Tomorrow Begins Today

The Grace of God

My grace is sufficient for you.

2 CORINTHIANS 12:9

The grace of God is like a multi-faceted diamond. One facet of grace is the help that allows us to endure bad times. It is God's grace that touches your life and lets you smile when the clouds are dark and gloomy.

Paul had a lot of experience when it came to bad things happening. He wrote, "We are hard pressed on every side, but not crushed; perplexed, but not in despair; persecuted, but not abandoned; struck down, but not destroyed" (2 Corinthians 4:8–9). We could say that he was down but not out. But what is it that made the difference? It was the grace factor that brought him comfort and help.

To describe grace simply as God's help would minimize it. But to understand that grace, which we do not deserve but is freely given, brings the answer to our great needs and connects us to the loving care of God. It's a discovery well worth making.

Today Can Be the Best Day of Your Life

A Challenge or a Handicap?

The soul of a lazy man desires, and has nothing;
But the soul of the diligent shall be made rich.

PROVERBS 13:4 NKJV

Scott Hamilton is the Olympic gold medal winner who earned the admiration of many for his 1984 performance at Sarajevo. But for ice skater Scott, it represented another kind of triumph as well.

When he was two years old, Scott stopped growing, afflicted by a childhood disease that almost cost him his life. But his stepparents encouraged his rehabilitation by teaching him to skate. For Scott, his problem was not a handicap but a challenge to overcome.

Helen Keller was not only born blind but deaf as well. In her day, the "deaf and dumb" were shunted to institutions where they lived a subhuman existence. But her indomitable spirit encouraged individuals not to quit or crawl into the corner of despair.

God has gifted each of us with abilities that can be explored to the depths. The real handicaps we face are lethargy, indifference, and the inability to shut off the TV and pick up a book and learn to read. The great handicaps are not the ones people are born with, but those that restrict "normal people" to a life of mediocrity and boredom.

Today Can Be the Best Day of Your Life

The Discipline of Prayer

You ask and do not receive, because you ask with wrong motives, so that you may spend it on your pleasures.

JAMES 4:3 NASB

*J*esus' disciples said, "Lord, teach us to pray" (Luke 11:1). They had prayed all their lives, but they concluded that they really did not know what prayer was all about.

If prayer is conversation between the child of God and his Father, we should note that in every conversation there is both expression (talking) and listening (hearing). Sören Kierkegaard observed, "A man prayed, and at first he thought he was talking. But he became more and more quiet until in the end he realized he was listening."

Openness, honesty, and trust mark a child's communication with his father. A child is not embarrassed to ask for the simple necessities of life, nor is he above talking to his father about his most personal needs. As a little child knows no limitations in asking, neither does our heavenly Father know any limitations in answering. "Call to Me and I will answer you, and I will tell you great and mighty things, which you do not know" (Jeremiah 33:3).

Today Can Be Different

Rejoice

Rejoice in the Lord always. I will say it again:
Rejoice!

PHILIPPIANS 4:4

A man plodding through life can "enjoy" a meal, the weather, or the company of friends, but only those with a heavenly connection can begin to fathom what it really means to "rejoice!"

In his powerful book *Jesus, Man of Joy*, Sherwood Eliot Wirt makes the point that in the life of the believer, joy is the result of a God-connection. "Jesus," he says, "was a man of such joy, such merriment, such gladness of spirit, such freedom and openness, that He was irresistible." This same joy is our birthright as God's children.

Joy is a powerful medicine for the healing of our lives, generated by the indwelling presence of God's Holy Spirit. Remember, as Paul told us, "the fruit of the Spirit is love, joy . . ." (Galatians 5:22). Unlike happiness, which is dependent on your circumstances—your health, your environment, your immediate world—joy can flood your heart no matter where you are or how you feel.

Today Can Be the Best Day of Your Life

Thy Will be Done

Thy kingdom come. Thy will be done in earth, as it is in heaven.

MATTHEW 6:10 KJV

Have you ever thought much about God's will in your life? Scores of people have never discovered that God has a will for them. Rather, they consider life as a game of chance, with a bit of luck and fate thrown in. Logic tells us that if Christ said we ought to pray for God's will, God must have a divine will for our lives—one that will give direction and guidance for living.

Here are three simple steps in finding God's will for your life: First, read your Bible. This is God's blueprint for living. You'll find direction for almost everything you'll ever face—it tells what God expects of us in our businesses, homes, and personal lives. Second, let circumstances guide you in finding that will. God gets blamed for a lot of things He's not responsible for. Third, sincerely pray for God's will and you will sense an inward witness from the Holy Spirit. Follow these steps, and the words "Thy will be done" will become a reality.

Today Can Be Different

How Could You Know How I Feel?

God sets the lonely in families, he leads forth prisoners with singing; but the rebellious live in a sun-scorched land.

PSALM 68:6

Do you think that because someone hasn't undergone the same problem as you then they cannot understand you? There would be few individuals to minister to our physical needs if doctors and nurses only treated people with medical problems that they themselves survived.

Think of Jesus—alone and without friends—as He faced forty days of testing in a desolate desert. Then, think of Him in the garden while facing one of the most difficult times of His life. He asked Peter, James, and John to join Him in prayer, but they fell asleep. Disappointed, Jesus asked, "Could you men not keep watch with me for one hour?" (Matthew 26:40).

Jesus experienced disappointment, loneliness, and abandonment. He was forsaken by family and friends. He even cried out, "My God, my God, why have you forsaken me?" (Matthew 27:46). There is someone who understands and who has been through the dark valley. He is Jesus. Take time to find Him.

Today Can Be the Best Day of Your Life

Christianity: Relevant or Not?

The one who does not love does not know God, for God is love.

1 JOHN 4:8 NASB

The Apostle John says that God's love prompted Him to do something almost unbelievable. In love, God embarked on a great project of redemption. In love, God sent His son, Jesus Christ, into the world to die for us and to save us from our sins (see also v.14).

John further points out that as we put our faith in Christ and His redeeming love, we are brought into fellowship with God (see v.15). John writes that through faith in the redeeming love of God we are "born of God" (I John 5:1) or born again.

If Christianity seems irrelevant to you, then you have not yet encountered Jesus Christ, who cannot only forgive your sins, but can also live within your heart and change your life. Come to Him and you will find the power and reality of His love in your life.

Today Can Be Different

I am Responsible

Therefore, strengthen your feeble arms and weak knees. "Make level paths for your feet," so that the lame may not be disabled, but rather healed.

HEBREWS 12:12-13

*W*illiam Wordsworth, the English poet, wrote, "The child is the father of the man." Events of your childhood shape your destiny and future as an adult.

We are the product of our genes and chromosomes, our heredity, and our environment. But the question is: "Must our future be determined by our past?"

We cannot erase our past. But the real issue is not where we came from, or even what happened to us as children or to our parents. The real issue is asking ourselves, "Where do I want to go? What do I want to become, and how do I want to reach my objectives?" The past may have been difficult, but the future is a new page. Dwelling on past failures or difficulties doesn't help us formulate a plan for advancement.

Long ago Paul wrote, "Forgetting what is behind . . ." (Philippians 3:13). Paul knew we would be thinking of that. "Let us fix our eyes on Jesus, the author and perfecter of our faith" (Hebrews 12:2). It's the upward look, not the backward glance, that gives us hope for tomorrow.

365 Guidelines for Daily Living

The Value of Human Life

*He who has the Son has life; he who does not
have the Son of God does not have life.*

1 JOHN 5:12

*W*hat is the value of human life?

Today, all around the world, armies of men and women—scientists, doctors, nurses, chemists, and researchers—show how highly they value human life by dedicating their own lives to sustaining it.

But how does God value human life? Consider these facts:

First, He created us. Science has done a great deal to preserve human life, but science cannot create life. Creation and life belong to God alone!

Second, He redeemed us through Christ. Jesus demonstrated that God is interested in saving human lives when He said, "I came that they may have life, and have it abundantly" (John 10:10 NASB).

"He who has the Son has life" said John in I John 5:12. Make sure you have the life that matters most —eternal life with God.

Today Can Be Different

The Faith of a Little Child

*I tell you the truth, anyone who will not
receive the kingdom of God like a little child
will never enter it.*

MARK 10:15

Our grandson William has worn glasses since he was a year old. One night, as their family were driving home, William looked out the window to find the moon. He asked, "Daddy, what's the moon made of?"

Donald replied, "It's made of rocks and dust, son. Astronaut James Irwin went to the moon and walked around on it, and that's why we know what it's made of. Do you remember that Astronaut Irwin held you in his arms when you were little?"

William thought for a few moments and said, "No, I don't remember. Is he dead, Dad?" Donald answered, "He's gone to heaven and he's with Jesus now."

William said, "Daddy, I don't think I'll recognize him in heaven." "Oh, yes," countered Donald. "Astronaut Irwin will say, 'Oh, I know you—you were the little boy I held in my arms at *Guidelines.'*"

William replied, "Then I'm going to sleep with my glasses in my hand from now on so I'll be able to recognize him!"

Is it any wonder that Jesus commended the faith of a little child?

365 Guidelines for Daily Living

Trouble

Yet man is born to trouble as surely as sparks fly upward.

JOB 5:7

Troubles come in all sizes, kinds, and descriptions. They are the result of living in an imperfect, sinful world. None are too good to be spared; none are too bad to be excluded from God's help when troubles come.

Stanley Collins, a Bible teacher and conference speaker, was felled by a heart attack. As he lay in the hospital thinking of the conferences he'd have to cancel, he began feeling sorry for himself. He asked, "Why me, God? Look at all these wonderful things that I am doing for you."

"Then," said Stanley, "it was almost as if I heard the echo of my own voice asking, 'Why not you?'"

When you step across the threshold and start asking, "Why not me?" you cease to make God your adversary and learn that He is your friend.

Everybody who faces trouble either becomes better or bitter because of it. Turn to the same source the psalmist turned to when he cried out, "The LORD is a refuge for the oppressed, a stronghold in times of trouble" (Psalm 9:9).

Today Can Be the Best Day of Your Life

Turning Pain into Gain

Before I was afflicted I went astray, but now I obey your word.

PSALM 119:67

Here are some guidelines that can help you when trouble knocks on your door:

GUIDELINE 1: Know that trouble is universal. Everybody faces adversity. Your attitude, though, has everything to do with how trouble affects you.

GUIDELINE 2: Realize that nothing in life is forever. Both blessing and adversity will not last.

GUIDELINE 3: Hold on to what you know is true, and refuse to believe what your emotions are telling you. You may think that God is punishing you or that you are suffering because of your inability to perform as well as others. Refuse to believe this. Go with what you believe, not with how you feel.

GUIDELINE 4: Focus on getting through the difficulties one problem at a time. Don't worry about everything all at once.

GUIDELINE 5: Let your adversity drive you to God. Trouble makes us realize our humanity, failure, and insufficiency in handling situations. It makes us realize that we need the Lord's help, His strength, His wisdom, and His guidance.

Today Can Be the Best Day of Your Life

What Trouble Does

You will keep in perfect peace him whose mind is steadfast, because he trusts in you.

ISAIAH 26:3

For the children of God, suffering and trouble take on different dimensions and confront us with different sets of parameters. We tend to think that because of our faith in God, we should be exempted from trouble.

But the rain and sunshine fall on both the just and the unjust. In the life of a believer, trouble should be regarded as that which God allows, to accomplish what might never be seen in this lifetime. That's where trust comes into the picture.

There are some things that have to be taken by faith. If we believe God is a loving Father, we must hold on to the promises of Scripture that tell us that God is in control of our lives and that Christ will not leave us nor forsake us.

In times of trouble, the faith of God's children is always put to the test. It is the promises of Scripture to which we must hold. When we trust our heavenly Father, we must yield to His hand, which controls the events of our lives.

Today Can Be the Best Day of Your Life

Putting Up with One Another in Love

You have heard that it was said, "Love your neighbor and hate your enemy." But I tell you: Love your enemies and pray for those who persecute you, that you may be sons of your Father in heaven.

MATTHEW 5:43–45

*A*nyone who denies that our natures are sinful has only to observe children. I recall an incident when I saw my sixteen-month-old grandson Andrew sipping Coke from a can with a straw. When his older brother took the can, Andrew promptly reached over and pinched the straw, cutting off the flow of Coke to his big brother. Who taught him to do that? He isn't old enough to talk, but he's old enough to fight!

C. S. Lewis wrote, "When you are behaving as if you loved someone you will presently come to love him. If you injure someone you dislike, you will find yourself disliking him more. If you do him a good turn, you will find yourself disliking him less."

Does it work? Indeed it does. Jesus urged us to do this very thing when He said, "Do to others as you would have them do to you" (Luke 6:31).

365 Guidelines for Daily Living

Ixthus

Today in the town of David a Savior has been born to you; he is Christ the Lord.

LUKE 2:11

Since the days Christians worshipped in the catacombs to avoid persecution, the fish has been a symbol of Christianity. Many throughout the world still display the fish on a lapel pin or a small insignia on the bumper of a car to indicate their faith as Christians. But what does the fish have to do with Christianity?

The Greek word for fish is *ixthus*. Five Greek letters form the word, and those letters form an acrostic that Christians clearly identified.

The first letter stands for *Iasous*, the Greek name for Jesus. The second letter represents *Christos*, the word translated "Christ." It is a title that meant "the anointed one."

The next two letters stand for *Theou Huios*, meaning "God's Son," reminding us of what John had written long ago: "God so loved the world that He gave His only begotten Son" (John 3:16 NKJV).

The final letter represents *Savior*, describing what Jesus did.

The *ixhtus* is a beautiful picture of who Jesus Christ is to us. Wear the symbol with pride.

365 Guidelines for Daily Living

June

THERE IS A TIME
FOR EVERYTHING AND A SEASON
FOR EVERY ACTIVITY
UNDER HEAVEN.

ECCLESIASTES 3:1

The Lord is a Refuge

Blessed are you when people insult you, persecute you and falsely say all kinds of evil against you because of me. Rejoice and be glad, because great is your reward in heaven.

MATTHEW 5:11–12

Martin Niemoeller, a former submarine captain turned pastor, spoke openly against Hitler. For this, Hitler sent him to prison. On February 7, 1938, Martin was to face his accusers in court.

A strange thing happened as Martin was led through an underground tunnel from prison to the courtroom. He suddenly heard the words of Proverbs 18:10: "The name of the LORD is a strong tower; the righteous run to it and are safe."

What alarmed Martin was that there was no one who could have spoken those words. Was this the audible voice of God speaking courage to a troubled heart?

They were from a Christian guard, who had learned that the tunnel acoustics could let someone's words be heard a considerable distance away. A fellow brother in Christ had wanted to encourage Martin.

Don't ever forget that the Lord is a fortress for the righteous and even whispering that truth to a down-trodden friend can make a difference.

Today Can Be the Best Day of Your Life

What's the Difference?

Salvation is found in no one else, for there is no other name under heaven given to men by which we must be saved.

ACTS 4:12

Suppose that you are walking through a jungle and come to a deep ravine. Looking over the side of the precipice you see raging waters below. You have to cross the chasm, but it seems there is no way across. Then you notice what appears to be a suspension bridge. It's woven from fiber and missing some of its bamboo reinforcements.

But you are a person of great faith. You are convinced that what you believe doesn't really matter provided you believe it with great intensity. Question: Will your strong faith get you across the weak suspension bridge? Of course not! Very weak faith in a strong bridge is far better than strong faith in a weak bridge.

The same kind of logic should apply to spiritual things. The issue is not how strongly you believe something but how strong the object of your belief is. What separates Christianity from all other religions of the world is one very strong point: the resurrection of Jesus.

The issue focuses on the empty tomb. If it is true that He did rise from the dead, then everything else He said and did is likewise true.

365 Guidelines for Daily Living

Going on Even When You Don't Feel Like It

Because of the LORD's great love we are not consumed, for his compassions never fail. They are new every morning; great is your faithfulness.

LAMENTATIONS 3:22–23

The most difficult part of the Christian experience is when the sky seems to fall and your world comes apart. At times like these, regardless of how you feel, hold on to the truth that God is still in control.

It's okay to tell Him that you don't understand, but don't measure God's goodness or faithfulness by the bad things that happen to you or the good things that happen to others.

Peter tells us to cast all our anxiety on Him because He cares for us (1 Peter 5:7). David says if we throw our burdens on the Lord, He will sustain us (Psalm 55:22).

Sometimes, just getting up in the morning and giving yourself a "kick start" isn't very glamorous, but it's what God requires. Getting the kids off to school, downloading the e-mail, dealing with the customer who is standing there tapping his credit card on the counter to get your attention—sometimes one hour or one task at a time is what God wants you to do.

Tomorrow Begins Today

Anxiety

*Before the mountains were brought forth, or even
thou hadst formed the earth and the world, even
from everlasting to everlasting, thou art God.*

PSALM 90:2 KJV

*A*nxiety is a form of worry, which has been called
"the acceptable sin of the saints" because so
many Christians are troubled by it. I freely admit that
on some occasions I find myself worrying about things,
letting it sap my energy, even when I know that my
concern cannot change a thing. But there are some
things I do that help me when I catch myself worrying,
and they will help you too.

The first thing I do is to remind myself that God is
sovereign, that He is in control. I look into the starry sky
and remind myself of the words of Scripture, "Before
the mountains were brought forth, or ever thou hadst
formed the earth and the world, even from everlasting
to everlasting, thou art God" (Psalm 90:2 KJV).

The second thing I do is to remind myself that God,
not worry, changes situations. The psalmist wrote, "Cast
your cares on the LORD and he will sustain you . . . "
(Psalm 55:22). I leave my burdens at the feet of our LORD.

365 Guidelines for Daily Living

What You Believe Makes a Difference

Now faith is being sure of what we hope for and certain of what we do not see.

HEBREWS 11:1

*U*nlike employers who make promises and don't keep them, or friends who forget what they tell you, God is never remiss on coming through with what He says He will do. Our faith in Him is founded on His character. Because people fail us, we often bring God down to their level, wondering if He really can be trusted as well. We forget the times when He has met us in the past.

Your earthly father may not be trustworthy, but your heavenly Father is. The Bible puts it pointedly: "God is not a man, that he should lie, nor a son of man, that he should change his mind. Does he speak and then not act? Does he promise and not fulfill?" (Numbers 23:19) And the obvious answer is, "No!"

The Quaker scholar David Elton Trueblood put it well when he said, "Faith is not belief without proof, but trust without reservation." Believing is important, but trusting is what brings the promises into our lives and our families. Real faith includes both.

Tomorrow Begins Today

"There Ain't No Light!"

Jesus once again addressed them: "I am the world's Light. No one who follows me stumbles around the darkness."

JOHN 8:12 TM

*M*any people identify with the words of Isaiah 59: "Like the blind we grope along the wall, feeling our way like men without eyes" (Isaiah 59:10). How do you know which way to go with your life when there are so many options? Two guidelines will help.

GUIDELINE 1: Recognize that Jesus Christ is the Light of the world. He said, "I am the way and the truth and the life. No one comes to the Father except through me" (John 14:6).

GUIDELINE 2: God's Word will give your life direction and purpose. The psalmist said, "Your word is a lamp to my feet and a light for my path" (Psalm 119:105).

What do you do when you've started on a journey and discover you've taken the wrong road? It happens a lot of time. Chances are you don't go back to your starting point. You make a change of direction to correct your error. That's how it is with God's will for your life. He renews you every day when you discover your need for Him to redirect your life.

Tomorrow Can Be Beautiful

If You Could Ask Just One Question

Consider therefore the kindness and sternness of God: sternness to those who fell, but kindness to you, provided that you continue in His kindness.

ROMANS 11:22

If you had an opportunity to ask God just one question, what would it be? I suspect your question would be more like one of these: "Why can't I have a baby when other women abort children they don't want?" or "Why was the life of my husband cut short?"

When your heart cries out, "Why?" remember these three guidelines:

GUIDELINE 1: God's nature is loving and kind—not harsh and capricious.

GUIDELINE 2: God is sovereign. Isaiah says, "Yet, O LORD, you are our Father. We are the clay, you are the potter; we are all the work of your hand" (Isaiah 64:8).

GUIDELINE 3: God cares what happens to His children. Your tears and cries are never ignored. When darkness seems to surround your life, realize that God experienced darkness when His Son faced death at Calvary. He's been where you are and He's with you now. And someday He'll answer your question.

Tomorrow Can Be Beautiful

It's My Nature to Worry

He who watches over you . . . will neither slumber nor sleep.

PSALM 121:3-4

Is worrying really wrong? No one can deny that there is plenty to worry about—the state of the economy, our health, domestic problems, and a lot of other things. Some even say it's in their nature to worry.

Jesus had a lot to say about this subject in the Sermon on the Mount (Matthew 5–7), where He talked about the birds that are fed by our heavenly Father. He chided the disciples for worrying about their clothes and food. In this passage, Jesus considered worry to be wrong because the worrier lacks faith in the power of his Heavenly Father to provide for His children.

How then should you deal with your worries? There is a solution to this problem. Simply put, it is learning to put into God's hands what you cannot change. Learning more about Him will give you confidence that He is able to take care of the storms in your life.

Remind yourself that He who created our world neither slumbers nor sleeps. He'll take the night shift and the day shift to follow. He never fails.

Today Can Be the Best Day of Your Life

Flowers Following the Fire

*God causes all things to work together for good
to those who love God.*

ROMANS 8:28 NASB

When fire swept through Laguna Canyon, a botanical garden containing more than 2,000 varieties of plants and flowers was destroyed. The fire blackened the hillside. Disaster? Yes! That's what people called it, and that it was. Yet, just five months later the hills were alive with the beauty of wild flowers that had not been seen in the area for nearly one hundred years.

At times what we consider to be a disaster is simply the hand of God rearranging and redirecting our lives. The difference between a Christian and the man who considers life to be a disorganized and disconnected move of fate, is that the Christian believes God's purpose and design is behind every event. He looks for the flowers after the fire.

If your life has been damaged by fire, let God speak peace to your heart, and begin to look for the flowers that can transform the blackened landscape. Allow the seeds that are only lying dormant to take full bloom.

Today Can Be Different

Trust and Obey

Remember your leaders, who spoke the word of God to you. Consider the outcome of their way and imitate their faith.

HEBREWS 13:7

*M*en and women who have made a mark for God share three common traits: 1) They respond without hesitation to the call of God in their lives; 2) Their simple faith is marked by complete obedience; and 3) They give what they have to the Lord completely and without reservation.

Stepping out in faith to trust God often puts us out of step with the crowd. When called a fool for what he was doing, Oswald Chambers responded, "I am not many kinds of fools in one; only one kind, the kind that believes and obeys God."

Faith demands a commitment of the heart, but obedience demands a commitment of your feet. Obedience does not require full knowledge of the game plan. It only requires confidence in the one you are following. For the child of God, obedience is not an option, it is a command. When we are confronted with a command, we have two choices: obey or disobey. There is no third option.

Tomorrow Begins Today

Frustration

"Never will I leave you; never will I forsake you."
HEBREWS 13:5

Our greatest frustrations in life are not usually mechanical. They are people-related, involving our family and the people we work with. They relate to the goals we set for ourselves, goals that are elusive and leave us hurting. They are often caused by situations we have no control over, or things that we wish had not happened but did.

Accept the fact that you cannot eliminate frustration in life. Do not think for a moment that if you are spiritual enough, or have enough faith, or pray enough, you will never be frustrated.

When we recognize, however, that the hand of God hovers over our lives in times of frustration as well as in times of blessing, we can then say, "God hasn't forsaken me; therefore, I will trust him to show me the way out of my frustration." Your attitude makes all the difference.

365 Guidelines for Daily Living

Even Spiritual Giants Get Frustrated

Those who live according to the sinful nature have their minds set on what that nature desires; but those who live in accordance with the Spirit have their minds set on what the Spirit desires.

ROMANS 8:5

*W*hat are some of the harmful responses to frustration? One is to get angry. That was Moses' response when the Israelites grumbled in the desert (Numbers 20).

Another option is to quit. You can pack up and go somewhere else. Essentially that was what Jonah did when God commanded him to go to Nineveh.

Another negative response to frustration is to anesthetize your pain, whether it is through drugs or alcohol. This, however, only creates more pain and never eliminates the frustration.

When we are frustrated, we tend to think that we are on our own, that God is either disinterested or too busy to care. But God *does* know our situations and He *does* care. Jesus Christ lived in a frustrating world.

God knows and cares. That is Good News!

365 Guidelines for Daily Living

In Times Like These

In the world you have tribulation, but take courage; I have overcome the world.

JOHN 16:33 NASB

Most of us would say it couldn't happen, yet on a number of occasions pilots have been known to disregard the instruments on their planes, and have flown directly into the ground. A pilot may become confused by cloud formations or from the motion of his plane. In his confusion, he momentarily loses his equilibrium and believes his instruments are wrong and he is right. In a state of confusion, he loses touch with reality, a mistake that can cost him his life.

In a world that is topsy-turvy politically, economically, and morally, it's no wonder many become confused and bewildered. In times like these, we need faith in God; that alone can give us security and steadfastness in a changing and turbulent world. The book of Hebrews speaks of this security as an "anchor of the soul, a hope both sure and steadfast" (Hebrews 6:19 NASB).

As you put your faith in God you can be assured of an anchor and a hope and a future.

Today Can Be Different

Thinking the Thoughts of Jesus Christ

Your attitude should be the same as that of Christ Jesus.

PHILIPPIANS 2:5

When an actor plays the part of another person, he tries to get inside the person's skin, to saturate himself with the person's thought processes, and to the extent possible, become that person. Can that really be done? Yes, say many professional actors.

Charlton Heston said that portraying Moses in the film *The Ten Commandments* greatly influenced his life. "Playing Moses," he said, "marked my life." To prepare for the role, Heston went to the Negev Desert of Israel, walked with the burning winds blowing sand in his face, and read what Moses wrote. He tried to think as Moses thought and to feel what he felt.

When Paul wrote to the Philippians, he urged them to strive to do the same thing with Jesus Christ. "Your attitude should be the same as that of Christ Jesus," says Philippians 2:5. Actually, the text can be translated, "Each of you should think the thoughts of Jesus Christ."

Have you ever noticed how people who have lived together for many years tend to think alike? Apply that insight to thinking the thoughts of Jesus.

Tomorrow Can Be Beautiful

Forgiveness

Though your sins are like scarlet, they shall be as white as snow; though they are red as crimson, they shall be like wool.

ISAIAH 1:18

Seven centuries before Christ, the prophet Micah exclaimed, "Who is a God like you, who pardons sin and forgives the transgression of the remnant of his inheritance? . . . You will . . . hurl all our iniquities into the depths of the sea" (Micah 7:18–19).

The significance of Micah's statement was not fully understood until recently, when oceanographers and hydrologists began to explore the depths of the ocean and discovered that life as we know it ceases to exist only a short distance beneath the surface.

When Micah says that God hurls our sins into the depths of the sea, he paints a beautiful picture of forgiveness. We can rest assured that the issue is settled, finished, never to be discussed again.

"Too easy!" you may be thinking. "Isn't there something else we must do?" The simple things are never easy. The most difficult thing we must do is acknowledge our need and realize that the solution to our sin is the grace of God, which brings forgiveness and restoration to everyone who believes.

Tomorrow Begins Today

Reaching Out to Others

The Lord is full of compassion and mercy.

JAMES 5:11

*W*hen Leslie C. Miller was chatting with an elderly surgeon friend, he asked, "Doctor, do you ever worry about the time when your fingers will lose their skills?" The doctor paused and then replied, "No . . . but I do confess that at times I worry that the day will come when I will no longer feel the suffering of my patients."

The doctor was describing compassion. The Greek word for compassion literally means to "suffer with someone." It means you feel what they feel—you hurt where they hurt.

Many of our problems could be solved if we could learn to feel the hurt when others hurt. Jesus did. When He was criticized for eating with tax-gatherers and sinners, Jesus replied, "It is not the healthy who need a doctor, but the sick" (Mark 2:17).

As a follower of Jesus, you should also be reaching out to the sick and lowly of this world. You wouldn't have to go very far to follow Jesus' example, for the world is full of hurting people. When you reach out, you will discover that healing comes to you as well.

Today Can Be the Best Day of Your Life

The Liberating Power of the Cross

But God forbid that I should glory, save in the cross of our Lord Jesus Christ, by whom the world is crucified unto me, and I unto the world.

GALATIANS 6:14 KJV

What Jesus did when He died at Calvary was to take your place, to die on your behalf so that you might be adopted into the family of God, so that our heavenly Father would accept His sacrifice in your stead. Does that make sense? The Cross is the foundation to the whole structure of faith, the key that opens the locked door to the very presence of God.

Long ago Isaiah explained, "But he was wounded for our transgressions, he was bruised for our iniquities: the chastisement of our peace was upon him; and with his stripes we are healed" (Isaiah 53:5 KJV).

The Cross provides the only rationale for God's forgiveness. It is the very heart of what Christ did, and we must never trivialize its power nor neglect its importance. It is the answer to the sinner's shame and bridges the gulf that separates us from the Father.

365 Guidelines for Daily Living

The Trouble with the World

"Come now, let us reason together," says the LORD.

ISAIAH 1:18

hen a magazine ran an article entitled, "What's Wrong with the World?" G. K. Chesterton responded with two words: "I am." Then he signed it, "Yours truly, G. K. Chesterton."

It's refreshing to hear someone like G. K. Chesterton say, "I am what's wrong with the world." Isaiah declared this a long time ago: "We all, like sheep, have gone astray, each of us has turned to his own way; and the LORD has laid on him the iniquity of us all" (Isaiah 53:6).

What's right about recognizing when you have been wrong? Plenty. Only when you acknowledge failure and sin is there hope that it can be forgiven and overcome. Acknowledging responsibility is the key to becoming a different person.

With our confession, followed by God's forgiveness, comes His redeeming help and strength to get on top of a situation that previously has controlled us. Chesterton was right. What's wrong with the world is ourselves! But God has the solution!

Tomorrow Begins Today

Is Ours a Pagan Society?

Some faced jeers and flogging, while still others were chained and put in prison. They were stoned; they were sawed in two; they were put to death by the sword.

HEBREWS 11:36-37

Has our culture become pagan? Compare the impact of the church on society now with that of a generation or two ago. To what degree are Christians impacting our society and our world? Or has Christianity simply become a reflection of our culture?

One of the greatest indictments against the church today is that it has become so accommodating that the line of demarcation between the church and the world has been all but rubbed out. It has become a mirror—not a spotlight.

If we genuinely mirror the gospel of Jesus Christ in our lives, our churches, businesses, homes, and marriages will be out of step with the surrounding culture. We will be thought of as radical religious fanatics just as certainly as the sun rises in the east and sets in the west. Remember what Jesus said to His disciples: "Woe to you when all men speak well of you, for that is how their fathers treated the false prophets" (Luke 6:26). A pagan culture will never be a friend to righteousness. That's just the way it is.

Tomorrow Begins Today

The Sparrow

Are not two sparrows sold for a penny? Yet not one of them will fall to the ground apart from the will of your Father.

MATTHEW 10:29

Of the more than 9,000 varieties of birds in the world, none is more common than the sparrow. Sparrows are pretty insignificant birds, yet it is amazing how they predominately find themselves in the language of the Bible. Jesus often spoke of sparrows to help people understand that God notices even them and that people are of far greater value than sparrows.

A lot of us can relate to the sparrows. We haven't climbed the Everests of success; we spend our lives down in the valley, going from one paycheck to the next, grubbing out an existence. We flit from one task to the next, doing the best we can with what we've got.

How beautiful it was that Jesus used the sparrow as an object lesson, which teaches us that we may not soar with the eagles or strut with the peacocks, but we are important to our heavenly Father.

The next time you hear the chirp of a sparrow or see one hopping from limb to limb outside your window, remind yourself that this most common of birds is important to our Heavenly Father. So are you.

Today Can Be the Best Day of Your Life

Real Friendship

A friend loves at all times.

PROVERBS 17:17

What is a friend? "A friend is a jewel that shines brightest in the darkness of misfortune," said one young woman. "A friend is a gold link," remarked a jeweler, "in the chain of life." Said a doctor, "A friend is a medicine for the ills of life."

A true friend is all of these, plus a great deal more. I've been musing on the qualities of friendship lately, and I am quick to say that God has blessed me with some faithful and dedicated friends. I've also concluded most of us have a lot of acquaintances, but not many real friends.

Real friendship isn't affected by social status, the economy, distance, or even time. With a real friend, you can pick up a relationship where you left it, no matter how far away you've been, or how long it's been since you were together. Real friendship isn't tarnished by money or the lack of it, nor is it enhanced by prestige and success. "If you love someone you will always believe in him, always expect the best of him, and always stand your ground in defending him" (see 1 Corinthians 13:7).

Today Can Be Different

Forgotten

*Why have you forgotten me? Why must I go
about mourning, oppressed by the enemy?*

PSALM 42:9

Have you ever felt that God has forgotten you, that He has allowed circumstances to shut you in a corner?

When Jesus Christ came to earth as a man, He proved that we have not been forgotten. For more than 400 years before His birth, there had been no open revelation—the heavens seemed to be sealed, and the darkness of man's loneliness seemed to be a prison. Then God reached down and touched humanity by sending His Son. This sacrifice demonstrates God's great concern for you and me.

The prophet Nahum wrote, "The LORD is good, a refuge in times of trouble. He cares for those who trust in Him" (Nahum 1:7). God can meet you at the point of your distress just as He has met thousands before. Sometimes we have to get to the end of ourselves to experience the firm, sure hand of God touching our lives with His presence. His touch may take on a thousand different forms. But you can be certain of one thing—when God touches your life, there will be no question that you have encountered the Divine.

Today Can Be the Best Day of Your Life

What are You Praying For?

*For this reason also, since the day we heard of it,
we have not ceased to pray for you and to ask that
you may be filled with the knowledge of His will
in all spiritual wisdom and understanding.*

COLOSSIANS 1:9

*P*aul wrote to the Colossians that he was praying that God would give them spiritual wisdom and understanding. Then from that would come the following:

1 They would walk in a manner worthy of the Lord and please Him by their lives (v. 10).

2 They would be strengthened by His might so that they would be steadfast, patient, and joyful (v. 11).

3 They might give thanks to the Father who had delivered them from the power of darkness and transferred them to the kingdom of His beloved Son, "in whom we have redemption, the forgiveness of sins" (vv. 12–14).

Many times in prayer we attempt to "use" God rather than to ask for wisdom and spiritual understanding that He might use us. We want Him to do for us whatever we ask rather than asking for His wisdom so that we can do whatever *He* asks.

How do you pray? For your life to be delivered in a neat little gift box, or do you, like Paul, ask for wisdom and understanding?

Today Can Be Different

Slow Down to Speed Up

Wait for the LORD; be strong and take heart and wait for the LORD.

PSALM 27:14

"Hurry and speed are great illusions," writes Winifred Peterson. "Contradictory as it may seem, *slowing down may be the best way to speed up.* . . . Slow down to decrease errors, to achieve accuracy, to reduce mistakes. Slow down and finish one thing, and then move on to the next. . . . Slow down and see the scenery instead of a blur. Slow down and wait upon the Lord. Often the best thing you can do is to do nothing until more light has revealed the way you should go."

Does waiting really help? Let me share a promise from Isaiah 40:31 (KJV): "They that wait on the Lord shall renew their strength . . . they shall run and not be weary; and they shall walk and not faint." This is the answer to the weariness and boredom of life today.

To wait on God means that you stop trying to work out the solution yourself. Quietly bow your heart before God and say, "Father, I do not know what to do. I need You to guide and direct me. Please take control of my life. Show me the path to take."

Today Can Be the Best Day of Your Life

When Suffering, Trust God

Though he slay me, yet will I trust in him.

JOB 13:15 KJV

"When we cannot trace God's hand," wrote Charles Haddon Spurgeon, "we can always trust God's heart." We all have times that confront us when we can see neither rhyme nor reason in what is happening. Why God allows the circumstances is not always clear.

When we have unanswered questions, we can curse God and blame Him—or turn to Him and let the trial drive us closer to Him. G. Campbell Morgan once said that any suffering would be bearable if we could only understand the reason for it. Yet faith is trusting Him —without doubt or bitterness—even when we cannot understand.

"Trust in the LORD with all your heart and lean not on your own understanding; in all your ways acknowledge him, and he will make your paths straight. Do not be wise in your own eyes; fear the LORD and shun evil. This will bring health to your body and nourishment to your bones" (Proverbs 3:5–8).

Today Can Be Different

From Faith to Faith

I thank my God through Jesus Christ for all of you, because your faith is being reported all over the world.

ROMANS 1:8

Have you ever faced a dark night of the soul? The heavens seemed brass, and your prayers seemed to rise no further than the sound of your voice. That God allows testing, which refines our lives, few would deny. The greater the testing, the greater the blessing.

In times like these, it's vital to hold on to what you know is true. You dare not yield a centimeter of ground to doubt, which bombards the soul. When I talk to someone who is going through drought in his or her spiritual life, I often say, "Tell me about the time you remember when God really broke through and did something in your life." Almost always you can remember at least once or twice when you felt that your prayers connected and God answered, right?

A period of spiritual drought lets the taproots of your soul go deeper into the Word of God, enabling you to understand more of His nature and purposes. The more you know of God's purposes in your life, the greater will be the measure of your trust and your portion of faith.

365 Guidelines for Daily Living

The Need to Belong

God setteth the solitary in families.

PSALM 68:6 KJV

On a downtown area one day, an unshaven ex-con walked up to a well-dressed businessman and said, "Sir, you look friendly," and with that, he began to tell the other man the sad story of his life. When he finished, he asked plaintively, "Will you do something for me?"

"Yes, if I can," replied the businessman.

"Well, sir," the man began, "not a soul in the world cares if I live or die. So would you mind just thinking about me for a couple of weeks? If I could think someone, somewhere was thinking about me as a human being, why—it would be worth so much to me."

Millions of people feel like this poor, lonely man. They long to feel loved, to really belong, to know that someone does care whether they live or die. But here is good news—through faith in Jesus Christ, we literally become "sons of God" (John 1:12 KJV). God becomes our Father and we become His children. And with this knowledge comes that good feeling of belonging.

Talk daily to Him. Share your joys and sorrows with Him. He, in turn, will share His peace, His love with you. And you will know that you truly belong.

Today Can Be Different

To Live Your Life Again

*Show me, O Lord, my life's end and the number
of my days; let me know how fleeting is my life.*

PSALM 39:4

In his book *Who Switched the Price Tags?* Tony
Campolo tells about a survey in which people over
age 95 were asked the question, "If you could live your
life all over again, what would you do differently?"

Most people wished they had risked more. For them
life had been too safe, too calculated. They wonder what
adventures they missed because they were fearful of
leaving security.

Others wished they had concentrated more on what
was really important. For them, life had been filled with
details of the routine.

The third category of people expressed the wish they
had done something worthwhile that would live on long
after they died.

"If you could live your life over again, what would
you do differently?"

In some cases, what's done is done. But in other cases,
what you would do if you could do it over again can yet
be done. It's never too late to begin anew. There's hope
for a better tomorrow.

365 Guidelines for Daily Living

The More Things Change, the More Nothing Changes

For the eyes of the LORD range throughout the earth to strengthen those whose hearts are fully committed to Him.

2 CHRONICLES 16:9

If there is one theme that runs throughout the historical books of the Bible, it is this: When people honor God, He honors them; and when people forget God and turn from Him, adversity eventually comes. The law of the harvest—a law that states that we reap what we sow—is as old as humanity.

Second Chronicles chapters 20 and 32 tell of two men, Jehoshaphat and Hezekiah. Both of these men faced annihilation from their enemies. But when they turned to God and threw themselves on His mercy, He miraculously intervened and spared them.

Be reminded of two things: First, understand that human nature never changes; and second, understand that God never changes either. He is the same yesterday, today, and tomorrow (Hebrews 13:8).

If there is one thing that the New Testament does, it brings us closer to God's help and makes His deliverance more personal.

Today Can Be the Best Day of Your Life

Peace in Our Lives

Peace I leave you; my peace I give you. I do not give to you as the world gives. Do not let your hearts be troubled and do not be afraid.

JOHN 14:27

*W*hat most people look for, but are unsure how to obtain, is peace. Here are several guidelines that can mean the difference between peace and turmoil:

GUIDELINE 1: Your old nature demands exoneration. Stop playing the "blame game" with your husband, wife, son, boss, or even yourself. It produces anger, irritation, and turmoil.

GUIDELINE 2: Get your relationship right with God. Talking with His disciples, Jesus said, "Peace I leave you; my peace I give you" (John 14:27). When your life is filled with bitterness, not much peace can fill your heart. Pray, "Lord Jesus, I have sinned. I need you to fix the problem of my heart. I want your forgiveness, and I want your peace." Christianity is more than preventive psychiatry; it is a gift that brings eternal life, and its by-product is peace.

GUIDELINE 3: Hold out the olive branch. Life is too short to live with broken relationships. You'll be amazed how different you feel when you say, "I'd like to be your friend. Let's settle this issue that has divided us."

Today Can Be the Best Day of Your Life

July

He made the earth by his power;
he founded the world by his
wisdom and stretched out the
heavens by his understanding.

JEREMIAH 51:15

The Greatest Sermon in the World

A large crowd of his disciples was there . . . and the people all tried to touch him because power was coming from him and healing them all.

LUKE 6:17,19

The world has seen great orators—from Demosthenes, Cicero, and Plato in the ancient world, to Abraham Lincoln and Winston Churchill in modern times. But no one will ever match the powerful message from the lips of Jesus Christ that we know as the Sermon on the Mount.

The Beatitudes are not simple words spoken to a large group of people in A.D. 26. Rather, they are timeless remedies for the sicknesses that tear our lives apart today. In the Beatitudes we find fundamental principles for our conduct, our attitude, and our spirit, which are the same needs in every generation.

Do yourself a favor. Take time to read Matthew 5–7 and listen for your name as God calls out to those who need a blessing.

Tomorrow Begins Today

Blessings or Last Rituals?

Now when he saw the crowds, he went up on a mountainside and sat down.

MATTHEW 5:1

When a large crowd of troubled, hurting folks came to see Jesus, believing that touching Him is the answer to their needs, He seated them on the grassy slopes of a mountain and taught them. We call the message The Sermon on the Mount. It is actually not a sermon, but teaching that brought them into confrontation with the resources of God. They walked away blessed and happy.

They wanted a quick fix; Jesus, instead, fixed the emptiness of their hearts, filling the void that can only be filled by a relationship with God.

Real happiness lies in learning those lessons Jesus taught long ago. We still haven't grasped what the book of Proverbs recorded: "There is a way that seems right to a man, but in the end it leads to death" (Proverbs 14:12). It is still true today.

Tomorrow Begins Today

Blessed are the Poor in Spirit

Blessed are the poor in spirit, for theirs is the kingdom of heaven.

MATTHEW 5:3

What did Jesus mean by the expression "poor in spirit"? Poverty of spirit and poverty of material things are not the same thing. Jesus is not saying that being financially poor is a great asset—not at all. What He is saying is that those who are destitute of resources and strength and who cannot help themselves are candidates for God to bring His kingdom to their hearts and blessing to their lives.

Poverty of spirit is the profound realization and admission that your resources are depleted, that you no longer have a quick fix or a simple solution, that there is no hope apart from God. Problem is, most of us find it difficult to accept that we are spiritually destitute, that we have exhausted our spiritual resources, and that God is our only hope.

But when you see yourself as poor in spirit and knock on heaven's door, you will be met by the Prince of Peace Himself who will not turn you away but will open the door and bless you. Jesus said it Himself, "Blessed are the poor in spirit, for theirs is the kingdom of heaven."

Tomorrow Begins Today

There Can be No Comfort Where there is No Grief

Blessed are those who mourn, for they will be comforted.

MATTHEW 5:4

Mourning and being blessed at the same time seem contradictory, but they're not. Simply put, there can be no comfort where there is no grief.

God promises to be "the God of all comfort" (2 Corinthians 1:3). We also find comfort in the promises of God's Word: "we through patience and comfort of the scriptures might have hope" (Romans 15:4 *KJV*). And, of course, we are comforted by friends and loved ones (see 1 Thessalonians 4:13–18).

Here are three simple guidelines that will help you work through grief.

GUIDELINE 1: Externalize your grief. Cry and tell someone about how you feel.

GUIDELINE 2: Internalize your faith. What your heart feels might challenge some things that your mind knows are true.

GUIDELINE 3: Eternalize your hope. Paul reminds the Thessalonians, who had lost loved ones, that Christ will return and our bodies will again rise from the grave (1 Thessalonians 4:13–18).

Tomorrow Begins Today

Is Meekness a Weakness?

Blessed are the meek, for they will inherit the earth.

MATTHEW 5:5

As meekness a weakness, something to be disdained? As Jesus taught the people on the mountainside, He candidly said, "Blessed are the meek, for they will inherit the earth" (Matthew 5:5). Modern translations usually render the word meek as "humble" or "gentle," but there is no trace of effeminacy or weakness in the word. Meekness speaks of gentleness of strength.

Jesus Himself was described as meek, and He had no agenda of His own. He had come only to do the will of His Father in heaven. When we consider ourselves "His to command," our strength comes under His control. In this position of weakness—or humbleness, if you prefer—we become candidates to inherit the earth.

Meekness may not be popular today, but it is exactly what we need.

Tomorrow Begins Today

Hungering and Thirsting for Righteousness

Blessed are those who hunger and thirst for righteousness, for they will be filled.

MATTHEW 5:6

Every person has needs that are fundamental to existence. Among the strongest are the physical yearnings for food and water. In the Sermon on the Mount, Jesus speaks of those two basic needs, but He applies them to a spiritual hunger and thirst for God: "Blessed are those who hunger and thirst for righteousness, for they will be filled" (Matthew 5:6).

Jesus says that your hunger and thirst for God will not go unmet—and He puts no conditions on this promise. He doesn't say, "Clean up your act, get spiritual, and then get in line for a blessing." He simply promises the blessing of fulfillment for those who hunger and thirst for righteousness.

Jesus says, "Come to me, all you who are weary and burdened, and I will give you rest. Take my yoke upon you and learn from me, for I am gentle and humble in heart, and you will find rest for your souls. For my yoke is easy and my burden is light" (Matthew 11:28-30).

Tomorrow Begins Today

Blessed are the Merciful

Blessed are the merciful, for they will be shown mercy.

MATTHEW 5:7

The Bible mentions the word mercy more than 370 times. Our great and awesome God is a God of mercy. "Rich in mercy" is the phrase Paul uses to describe God in Ephesians 2:4—in stark contrast to pagan gods whose wrath had to be satisfied, often with human blood. Anthropologists would agree that mercy was not a common attribute of pagan deities.

Although God's mercy has been shown from generation to generation, there is an end to it. Remember before the Flood, God said, "My spirit shall not always strive with man" (Genesis 6:3 KJV). But the door is still open. As Peter put it, "Anyone who asks for mercy from the Lord shall have it and shall be saved" (Acts 2:21 TLB). Jesus says, "Blessed are the merciful, for they will be shown mercy" (Matthew 5:7). As children of God, we must strive to reflect a merciful attitude with our children, business colleagues, friends, and associates. Make mercy a garment which you drape over friends and enemies alike.

Tomorrow Begins Today

Blessed are the Pure in Heart

Blessed are the pure in heart, for they will see God.

MATTHEW 5:8

The brain may be the center of the intellect, but it is the heart that captures the interest of lovers and poets. It is your heart, not your head, that reveals the kind of person you are. When Jesus taught a multitude on the mountainside, He pronounced a special blessing on those whose hearts are pure. "Blessed are the pure in heart," He said, "for they will see God" (Matthew 5:8).

Becoming pure in heart is not an easy road; it is a lifestyle and a choice that sets your feet on a path that leads to God.

Life at its longest is short, very short, and sooner or later we all face eternity. When Jesus says that the pure in heart shall see God, He affirms the reality of heaven and affirms that the crown of life lies within the grasp of the smallest, the least significant, and the poorest among us. It belongs to any person whose heart is pure and upright before God.

Tomorrow Begins Today

Blessed are the Peacemakers

Blessed are the peacemakers, for they will be called sons of God.

MATTHEW 5:9

Have you noticed how much easier it is to wage war than to make peace?

Not only is it hard to keep the peace, but it's even more difficult to make peace where there is none, to mediate between angry and hostile individuals.

"Sons of God" is the title that Jesus gives to the peacemakers of the world. If a son reflects the image of his father, surely we can see the nature and character of our heavenly Father in those who broker peace. Not only is God described as "the God of peace" five times in the New Testament, but He desires that His children be peacemakers as well.

The writer of Hebrews says it well when he writes, "May the God of peace, who through the blood of the eternal covenant brought back from the dead our Lord Jesus, that great Shepherd of the sheep, equip you with everything good for doing his will, and may he work in us what is pleasing to him, through Jesus Christ, to whom be glory for ever and ever. Amen" (Hebrews 13:20–21).

Tomorrow Begins Today

Rejoice and be Glad

*Blessed are those who are persecuted because
of righteousness, for theirs is the kingdom
of heaven.*

MATTHEW 5:10

*T*he person who stands for nothing will fall for anything. But even the person who does stand for something—who has the conviction to abide by what he
believes is right—will soon discover that not everyone
appreciates his commitment to decency.

How should we respond when we become targets of
hostility or persecution for doing right? The following
guidelines may help:

GUIDELINE 1: Pray for your enemies. Remember that
Saul of Tarsus, the archenemy of the early church,
later became the Apostle Paul.

GUIDELINE 2: Realize that Satan is using those who
oppose you. Be on your guard. Put on the full armor of
God and stand strong and true.

GUIDELINE 3: Remember that the opposition is not
forever.

GUIDELINE 4: Rejoice and be glad. Thank God that
His grace is sufficient for your need.

No one welcomes hostility or persecution for doing
right, but when we endure, we are blessed and counted
worthy of the kingdom of heaven.

Tomorrow Begins Today

Faith's Foundation

Faith comes from hearing the message, and the message is heard through the word of Christ.
ROMANS 10:17

At the end of World War II, in one of the Nazi concentration camps, some Allied soldiers found a Star of David carved into a wall with these words beneath it: "I believe in the sun—even when it does not shine. I believe in love—even when it is not shown. I believe in God—even when He does not speak."

How can we have that kind of faith?

First, we must realize that faith is necessary no matter how dark the hour.

Second, our faith must be simple. Jesus used the illustration of the simplicity of a child's faith to help His disciples understand faith.

Third, we must believe in the power of God. Our faith is only as valid as its object, and the object of our faith is God and His limitless power.

Fourth, we must wait for the reward of faith. Some say that God no longer does the miraculous, and for them, nothing much miraculous ever happens. But for those who simply trust God, it is amazing what happens. Faith does makes a difference.

Tomorrow Begins Today

The Power of Time

Why, you do not even know what will happen tomorrow. What is your life? You are mist that appears for a little while and then vanishes.

JAMES 4:14

What can bring down empires, humble the mightiest of men, crumble a craggy granite peak, and, yet has the power to heal a wound and change a life? Described as the greatest power on earth, that force is time.

There are many inequalities in life. But when it comes to time, everybody gets the exact same allotment: twenty-four hours a day, no more and no less.

Every morning you are credited with 186,400 seconds, and it's up to you to use it or lose it. At the end of the day, whatever you haven't used is lost forever. The fragile fleeting nature of time led Moses to pray, "Teach us to number our days, that we may apply our hearts unto wisdom" (Psalm 90:12 KJV).

How have you used the time that God has given you? He has given each of us a measure of time, and when we are done, He will ask us to account for how we utilized it.

Tomorrow Can Be Beautiful

If I Can Just Get Through This Problem

Don't worry about anything; instead, pray about everything.

PHILIPPIANS 4:6 TLB

f I can just get through this problem, I'm sure every-thing will be okay." Ever think that? You grit your teeth and get through your problem only to find that several more have cropped up on the horizon. It's like pedaling a bicycle. Going uphill is so slow and takes so much energy, and then the downhill run turns quickly into another uphill climb.

The word translated "worry" or "anxiety" in the New Testament is interesting. Paul used it when he described his care for the churches. Yet he also used the word when he advised believers not to be overwhelmed by an immediate problem but rather to pray and commit it to the Lord (Philippians 4:6).

Jesus also spoke of earthly worries. "In this world you will have trouble," He said. But He didn't stop there. He continued, saying, "But take heart! I have overcome the world" (John 16:33). Concentrate on finding His strength and power, and learn from the experience you are working through right now.

Today Can Be the Best Day of Your Life

Putting Something into Worship

My mouth will speak in praise of the Lord.
Let every creature praise his holy name for ever
and ever.

PSALM 145:21

$\mathcal{M}$any of us confuse blessing and worship. A blessing is not something you do; it is something you receive. Worship is what you do, and the blessing of the Almighty follows the act of true worship.

The word *blessing* is not an easy word to define in English. The Greek word which the New Testament uses is sometimes translated "happy," but it is far more than a feeling of light frivolity. It bears the idea of sense of well-being, of having received something of the nature and expression of the Almighty. It is the warmth which comes as the result of a father's smile, the sense of well-being which a mother generates as she holds her infant in her arms.

In relation to God, His blessing is the result of His goodness and mercy to us. It is the warmth of His presence when we have recognized His true greatness and respond to it. But be quite certain: Worship comes first, then His blessing follows.

365 Guidelines for Daily Living

Getting to Know God

Do you not know? Have you not heard? The LORD is the everlasting God, the Creator of the ends of the earth.

ISAIAH 40:28

Many individuals know something about God but do not know Him personally. They understand that there is some kind of a connection between creation and the Almighty Creator. But they wonder, "Can I really know God?"

You can, but you've got to look for the answers in the right place. You see, reading a book on cooking will never help you be a good chef. Reading a book on royalty isn't the same as a face-to-face audience with Queen Elizabeth II of Britain.

That's why you need to go to the only real source which answers the question, "How can I know God?" It is the Bible. This book says you can know God personally through His Son Jesus Christ. The Cross became a bridge for us to know God and to become His children.

You are no accident. You are a person created in the image of God. You are one of a kind among the billions of people who live on planet Earth, and it is God's desire to bring you into a relationship with Himself. Don't settle for anything less than knowing God.

365 Guidelines for Daily Living

Translating Dreams into Reality

That I may know Him, and the power of His resurrection and the fellowship of His sufferings, being conformed to His death.

PHILIPPIANS 3:10 NASB

"If wishes were horses, beggars would ride and kings would walk," says the old aphorism. There's a vast difference between wishing or dreaming, though, and translating those dreams into reality. A vagrant may lie in a clover field and wish he were riding in a jet, but unless he's willing to roll up his sleeves and go to work, he will never translate that wish into reality.

What about the things you've been hoping to do someday? The Apostle Paul said that if you want to translate your dreams into realities, decide what it is you want to accomplish and then stay with the job. "This one thing I do" (Philippians 3:13 KJV), he said.

Paul had decided what *one thing* he wanted to accomplish: "That I may know Him and the power of His resurrection and the fellowship of His sufferings, being conformed to His death" (v. 10).

Determine to find God's direction for your life and when you find it, you'll stumble across fulfillment and purpose.

Today Can Be Different

Make It a Habit

But you were washed, you were sanctified, you were justified in the name of the Lord Jesus Christ and by the Spirit of our God.

1 CORINTHIANS 6: 11

*A*re you a victim of your habits? Or can you change your habits and lifestyle? Habits can be broken, but it takes strong motivation, something stronger than the force of habit, to create change.

The following guidelines can make a difference in your life:

GUIDELINE 1: Break the old habit decisively. Don't cut off a dog's tail an inch at a time. The Ephesians burned their magic books in one great fire. Draw a line, cross it—and by the grace of God, never return.

GUIDELINE 2: Establish a new habit immediately. "In the main," wrote Henry James, "all experts agree that abrupt acquisition of a new habit is the best way."

GUIDELINE 3: Go public with your commitment. Tell your friends. Sign a pledge. Paint a sign, or fly a banner, but don't go back.

GUIDELINE 4: Reach out for God's strength. The Bible is full of promises of help. The Holy Spirit within you supplies the strength you need to be the person He wants you to be. He makes the difference.

Tomorrow Can Be Beautiful

Come on, Let's Reason Together

But if you do not forgive men their sins, your Father will not forgive your sins.

MATTHEW 6:15

Have you ever wondered why some people refuse to forgive, why they hold on to bitterness until it becomes a cancer that eats away at them? Medical research has proven conclusively that people who are free of bitterness and anger live longer and enjoy life more than those who refuse to forgive. There's no logic in living with bitterness.

The bottom line is that releasing bitterness, giving up your right to hurt someone else because that person hurt you, is not only good for your health, but good for your heart and soul as well. The best way to deal with those who hurt you is to forgive them, love them, and let God deal with them in His way, and in His time.

Have you forgiven those who hurt you? Jesus said that unless we forgive others, our Father in heaven will not forgive us. So, since you are in need of forgiveness yourself, you had better learn to forgive. Say it, write a letter, make a telephone call—whatever is necessary —just do it. You'll be the winner when you do.

Tomorrow Begins Today

Be Still, and Know that I am God

Be still before the LORD, and wait patiently for Him.

PSALM 37:7

Nothing makes us more helpless than being in the position of having played out all our options. During this time, there is nothing more we can do except trust God.

About 3,000 years ago, God addressed this issue when He said, "Be still, and know that I am God" (Psalm 46:10). The translation of "be still" means, "relax, let go, stop pushing."

Is anything so contrary to our nature? Yet there are times and situations that are beyond our scope and power to fix, and it is then that God says, "Be still, and know that I am God."

Notice that God doesn't just tell us to "Be still" but adds a second command: "Know that I am God." Meditation or being quiet may have some therapeutic value. Taking time out from a busy schedule never hurts anyone, but just slowing down isn't enough. Understanding that God is God gives meaning to what would otherwise be a hopeless situation.

Today Can Be the Best Day of Your Life

David and Depression

*Why are you downcast, O my soul? Why so
disturbed within me? Put your hope in God, for I
will yet praise him, my Savior and my God.*

PSALM 43:5

*W*hen people get depressed, no matter what has caused their depression, they feel so alone and think that nobody has ever been in a hole quite as deep as theirs.

In Psalms 42 and 43, the writer—probably David—pours out his discouragement. He uses words such as *tears, despair, mourning, weeping, cast down, depressed* and so forth. Then he gives his solution for dealing with depression God's way.

GUIDELINE 1: Pour out your heart to God.

GUIDELINE 2: Remember what God has done for you.

GUIDELINE 3: Make the decision in your heart to praise the Lord.

GUIDELINE 4: Focus on God rather than on what depresses you.

GUIDELINE 5: Pray for God's light and truth.

GUIDELINE 6: Verbalize your faith. Both Psalms 42 and 43 end with a reaffirmation of faith and trust in God.

God's psychiatry lifts us from depression and brings peace to despairing hearts.

365 Guidelines for Daily Living

The Big Picture

I know that everything God does will endure forever; nothing can be added to it and nothing taken from it. God does it so that men will revere Him.

ECCLESIASTES 3:14

Following the devastating Great Fire of London in 1666, the English architect and scientist Sir Christopher Wren designed many of the eighty-seven churches that needed rebuilding.

When Wren was visiting one of the buildings under construction, he asked several workers what they were doing. One replied, "I'm a stonemason. I'd think that's pretty obvious."

Another man, perched on a scaffold above the floor of the building, answered differently. He said, "I'm helping Sir Christopher Wren build a cathedral."

Both men were working on the cathedral, but only the second man saw the big picture. Seeing the big picture is always the challenge, whether you're a laborer, a CEO, a mother, or a secretary.

At times it will seem that your work is unnoticed and unappreciated. At times you'll feel that what you do doesn't matter. Don't lose sight of the big picture. Remember, you are doing something for God and He notices. Our reward ultimately comes from the Lord.

Tomorrow Begins Today

Meditation

I meditate on your precepts . . . I will not neglect your word.

PSALM 119:15A, 16B

How many people do you know take even five minutes a day to meditate on spiritual matters?

Rich benefits are in store for us when we, as God's children, meditate long enough to remember what He has done. We understand that the problems of life aren't nearly as great as our heavenly Father, and we begin to have hope and peace of mind.

To help you develop the practice of meditating on the things of the Lord, here are some suggestions:

1 Focus on God's Word. The best way to do this is to memorize Scripture verses and quote these for yourself.

2 Take a few moments and think about the nature and character of God. Focusing on His greatness, His majesty and His great love for you will dwarf your problems and bring life into perspective.

3 Meditate on what God has done for you personally. You will be amazed at how your attitude changes when you lift your heart to praise God. It is when we meditate upon Him that we hear His voice and know that He is God.

Today Can Be the Best Day of Your Life

Personal Crisis

When you pass through the rivers, they will not sweep over you. When you walk through the fire, you will not be burned.

ISAIAH 43:2

Nobody likes to face a crisis. We reason that godly men are so on top of things that they just don't have the same problems as others have. The truth is that all people face the fire and deep waters. There are, however, special provisions for God's children who face these problems.

The beginning of Isaiah 43 reads: "Fear not, for I have redeemed you; I have called you by your name; you are Mine!" (Isaiah 43:1 NKJV). Don't forget God loves you. He may well have allowed the experience that has you backed up to the wall or left you lying flat on a hospital bed because He wants to do something in your life that just couldn't happen apart from difficult circumstances. God explains that He allows tough circumstances because His children are "precious in His sight" (see Isaiah 43:4). How much more important to know this than to be exempt from trials and to wonder if the bridge over which we must cross is strong enough to hold us.

Today Can Be Different

"Give Yourself"—Jesus

If anyone would come after me, he must deny himself and take up his cross daily and follow me. For whoever wants to save his life will lose it, but whosoever loses his life for me will save it.

LUKE 9:23-24

While Socrates became famous for his dictum, "Know thyself," Jesus Christ lived the admonition, "Give thyself." There is a great difference between knowing yourself and giving yourself.

Knowledge of self is important, but often we aren't happy once we get to know ourselves. Instead, Christ said, "Give thyself!" In giving, we receive, and in dying we live. Jesus said, "If anyone would come after me, he must deny himself and take up his cross daily and follow me. For whoever wants to save his life will lose it, but whosoever loses his life for me will save it" (Luke 9:23, 24).

The beautiful thing about giving yourself, first to God then to others, is that your old self will change. Paul described it as becoming "a new person." Yes, it is important to know yourself—your weaknesses, failures and sins. But once you know that, do something about it. Give yourself and become the person God wants you to be.

Today Can Be the Best Day of Your Life

Passing Through Deep Waters

When you pass through the waters, I will be with you; and through the rivers, they will not overflow you. When you walk through the fire, you will not be scorched, nor will the flame burn you.

ISAIAH 43:2 NASB

A lot of folks—maybe you're included—can accept the fact that God is a God of concern, but they wonder how much of the time He's in control. They can accept, "If it's good, it must be of God!" but they also reason, "If times are tough, I must have missed God somewhere!"

In chapter 43 Isaiah recorded words that still bring a great deal of comfort. "When you pass through the waters, I will be with you; and through the rivers, they will not overflow you."

God says, "I will be with you," and those five words should make all the difference in the world. And if that's not enough, they're followed by two other statements. God says, "You are honored, and I love you" (Isaiah 43:4). Wow! That's good news! We could only face all the battles of life victoriously with the certainty that He is with us.

Today Can Be Different

Revenge, Repression, or Forgiveness?

For if you forgive men when they sin against you, your heavenly Father will also forgive you. But if you do not forgive men their sins, your Father will not forgive your sins.

MATTHEW 6:14-15

When you are victimized by wrongdoing, you choose any of these three responses: revenge, repression or forgiveness.

Most people choose revenge. But violence only begets more violence, and the cycle is unending. It results in continued pain and anger.

The second response to wrongdoing is to repress how you feel about the incident. But repression doesn't work. Like a dormant volcano, it eventually erupts with a deadly spew that poisons life.

The third response is forgiveness. When you forgive someone, you release the anger and hostility and let God deal with the wrong. In due time, God will enforce His divine justice, for Scripture says, "'Vengeance is Mine; I will repay,' saith the Lord" (Romans 12:19).

Today Can Be the Best Day of Your Life

Solitude

And everyone went to his home . . . Jesus went to the Mount of Olives.

JOHN 7:53-8:1

Solitude, who needs it? Is it just a waste of time, or does it meet a need?

Psychologist James McConnel said that periods of solitude allow a person to file away his experiences in his mind and let him sort things mentally. He considers it as a kind of mental housecleaning, a time of quietness simply to think.

Different people meet that need in different ways. American businessman and statesman Bernard Baruch used to take time from his busy schedule each day to go to the park and feed the pigeons. Wasted time? No, it was his time to think without interruptions.

Christ Himself repeatedly withdrew from the crowds to find a place of solitude to pray. It was His time to fellowship with His Father. Likewise, every believer should take time from each day's schedule to spend time in the presence of his heavenly Father. Start each day with ten minutes of prayer and meditation on the Word of God. After one week, look back and analyze the time spent. Then decide whether it was time wasted—or the most profitable ten minutes of your day!

Today Can Be Different

Handling Time and Stress

We must work the work of him who sent me.

JOHN 9:4

*P*eople have a need for intimate communication. Aside from this, there is also a need for us to know how handle the demands on our time.

Jesus lived with a sense of purpose few understand. He never seemed to be in a hurry. He never traveled more than a few hundred miles altogether. Yet, Jesus revealed a secret that is indeed the answer to all of our time-and-stress-related problems today. Everything that consumed Him—activities, travel, and relationships —He submitted to His Father. "Not my will, but yours be done," Jesus prayed (Luke 22:42).

If we submit every aspect of our lives to the Lordship of Jesus Christ, life will take on a new dimension. It's then only a matter of determining what God would have us do at any given time.

Most of us are trying to do more than God intends, but there is a better way—His way.

Today Can Be Different

Meet Mr. Peter

Peter, an apostle of Jesus Christ . . . Grace and
peace be yours in abundance.

1 PETER 1:1-2

*M*eet Mr. Simon Peter. Oh, some folks put a halo over him and call him St. Peter, and some history books use his Aramaic name and call him Cephas. Jesus gave him the name Peter, meaning "Rock."

As I think of Peter, I think of his four qualities.

• First, he was a man of action. He never hesitated.

• Second, Peter was a man of commitment and loyalty.

• Third, Peter was a man of courage.

• Lastly, he was a man of conviction.

"I say You are the Son of God!" shouts Peter as he waves his fist in the air to drive home his point. According to tradition Peter requested that he be crucified upside down, because he did not deem himself worthy to die as his Lord had died.

Peter was a changed individual, his forceful character found expression in a different cause, that of changing the world. The God who changed his life is still in the business of changing people.

365 Guidelines for Daily Living

How Valuable are You?

For the Son of Man came to seek and to save what was lost.

LUKE 19:10

*M*uch of what Jesus said when He taught the multitudes was about how valuable people are. In the book of Luke are parables which illustrate this. There were one hundred sheep; one was lost. There were ten coins; one was lost. There were two sons; one was lost.

The person who struggles with feelings of inadequacy, who feels as if he is never good enough to warrant and receive God's love, is pictured in these stories. Yet what that person doesn't understand is that God is far more interested in his coming to the Father than he is in being found by the Father. When we were lost, Jesus Christ came seeking and searching. Isaiah wrote, "We all, like sheep, have gone astray, each of us has turned to his own way" (Isaiah 53:6). But Jesus said, "For the Son of Man came to seek and to save what was lost" (Luke 19:10).

There is help for your confusion and hope for your despair. Take time to read these three parables in Luke 15, and see yourself in that which was lost.

Today Can Be the Best Day of Your Life

The Commitment of Faith

Commit everything you do to the Lord. Trust him to help you do it and he will.

PSALM 37:5 *TLB*

Faith has two elements: belief and trust. Belief deals with knowledge—facts that you accept as true. Belief is intellectual assent to truth. On the other hand, trust deals with action. It involves commitment to what you intellectually accept as truth.

Both elements are absolutely necessary. Notice, first of all, that believing in something requires knowing that something. Obviously, what we could see first-hand, we would believe. But believing is only part of faith—it is not complete until you believe something to the point of commitment.

When it comes to your faith in God, it is very easy to have only belief in God. It is easy to believe that God exists—in fact, many people believe in His existence today. But even believing that God loves man enough to send His Son does not mean that your faith is complete. Only when you not only believe but trust Him as well can you confidently say, "My Lord and my God."

If your faith in God is to be complete, you must not only believe, but you must be willing to trust Him as well. That's true faith.

365 Guidelines for Daily Living

August

NOW HE WHO SUPPLIES SEED
TO THE SOWER AND BREAD FOR FOOD
WILL ALSO SUPPLY AND INCREASE
YOUR STORE OF SEED AND WILL
ENLARGE THE HARVEST OF YOUR
RIGHTEOUSNESS.

2 CORINTHIANS 9:10

According to Your Faith

"What do you want me to do for you?" "Lord, I want to see," he replied.

LUKE 18:41

As Jesus was leaving Jericho, on His way to Jerusalem, He encountered two blind men. The blind men had heard that He could heal the sick and deformed. They cried out to Jesus: "Have mercy on us, Son of David!" When Jesus heard this, He stopped. "Do you believe that I am able to do this?" Jesus asked them, and they replied, "Yes, Lord." According to Matthew, who was an eyewitness, Jesus touched them and said, "According to your faith will it be done to you!"

So often, Jesus did things that were the opposite of human logic. The Jews placed a premium on action, but Jesus required faith. Look again at the question that Jesus asks: "Do you believe that I am able to do this?" What's your answer? Faith is simply believing what the Word says. It doesn't attempt to understand how God does it. It just believes that He can.

Faith does not deny the problem. It just believes that God is powerful and that He will honor the promises He has made.

Tomorrow Can Be Beautiful

Handling Interruptions

Many rebuked him and told him to be quiet, but he shouted all the more, "Son of David, have mercy on me!" Jesus stopped and said, "Call him."

MARK 10:48–49

ow do you view life's interruptions? As Jesus started for Jerusalem, a blind man called Bartimaeus called out to Jesus and begged Him for mercy. This man had no social status, no education, and no money. Day after day, he lived on the charity of passersby. Yet everything stopped for Jesus' encounter with somebody who was a nobody.

This incident forces me to re-examine my perspective. Would I have said, "Get out of my way, blind man, I'm on my way to Jerusalem to save the world"? Probably. Is it possible that I could save myself a lot of headaches if, at the beginning of the day, I prayed, "Lord, what do You want me to do today?" instead of saying, "God, bless my schedule and help me to get done all the wonderful things I've planned"?

My response to interruptions can only be different when I relinquish what I want to do to our heavenly Father and say, "OK, Lord, this interruption must be part of Your plan, so please help me to respond without irritation. For Your sake, Amen."

365 Guidelines for Daily Living

God Has a Plan

For I know the plans I have for you . . . plans to prosper you . . . to give you a future and a hope.
JEREMIAH 29:11

God has a plan, but chance has no part in it. Take, for example, planet Earth—this sphere spins on its axis at a speed of 1,000 miles per hour and hurtles through space at 27,000 miles per hour. If our planet were closer to the sun, we could not stand the heat; if it were further away, we could not stand the cold.

Understanding God's plan for nature helps me realize that He has a plan for my life as well. You might be thinking, "You don't know how messed up my life is! How could God possibly have a plan for my life?"

You may have heard this before: "Man's extremity is God's opportunity!" What you see as chaos, God views as an opportunity. You, my friend, are of greater value than the stars in heaven.

Are you discouraged? Then listen to the still voice of God saying, "For I know the plans I have for you, plans to prosper you and not to harm you, plans to give you hope and a future" (Jeremiah 29:11).

Today Can Be the Best Day of Your Life

Encouragement

If therefore there is any encouragement in Christ . . . make my joy complete by being of the same mind.

PHILIPPIANS 2:1-2 NASB

*W*hen you listen to words of encouragement, your spirit perks up and your whole attitude takes on an uplifted stance. But when you allow words of discouragement to penetrate your heart, your attitude becomes pessimistic.

Much of life seems to be working against us, and that's not pessimism—it's a realistic observation. For every person who pats us on the back, there are nine others who clobber us. Therefore we have to cultivate the attitude of encouragement. The habit of encouragement has to be learned. It doesn't come naturally.

A couple recently came to me for counsel. After listening to a recital of petty woes and failures, I gave them an assignment for the next session. "Make a list of all the things you admire in each other." It was a changed couple that returned, each admitting they hadn't known the other really admired them. It had been easier to emphasize each other's faults.

Encouragement strengthens the heart and puts resolve in our actions. It can make the difference between success and failure, sunshine and gloom.

Today Can Be Different

Shortcut to Happiness

*And let the peace of God rule in your hearts,
to which also you were called in one body;
and be thankful.*

COLOSSIANS 3:15 NKJV

Almost 300 years ago the English writer William Law wrote about a shortcut to happiness. "If anyone would tell you the shortest, surest way to happiness and all perfection, he must tell you to make it a rule to yourself to thank and praise God for everything that happens to you. For it is certain that whatever seeming calamity happens to you, if you thank and praise God for it you will turn it into a blessing."

Learning to praise and thank God for everything is an expression of your faith. Your act of thanking God for everything that happens proves that you believe God is alive and that it is He, not chance or fate, that really is in control of your life.

Praising God for what happens does not necessarily mean that you understand why everything happens. When your heart cries out "Why?" God often says, "Just trust Me."

William Law, like untold thousands before him, discovered that praising God for His workmanship in life will bring joy and happiness. Start right now by thanking Him for His goodness to you.

Today Can Be Different

Successful and Significant

Here is the conclusion of the matter: Fear God and keep his commandments, for this is the whole duty of man.

ECCLESIASTES 12:13

Three of the most important questions that will ever confront you are 1) Where do you want to go with your life? 2) How are you going to get there? And 3) Once you have arrived, what are you going to do? The first question deals with your goals, the second with your ethics, and the third, your significance as a person.

Some people are content simply to survive in life. They do as little as possible. They exert minimal input, they are satisfied with minimal reward.

The next group are the ones who have clearly defined goals and reach them. But having reached their goals, many of these dynamic, successful people find that life still has no purpose or meaning for them.

The third group aspires for significance. Not necessarily wealthy or famous, they touch the lives of others in such a way that our world becomes a better place. They are the ones who see a need and fill it.

No one is ever really happier than when he or she rises to the level of significant living. That's how God designed us.

365 Guidelines for Daily Living

Binding the Strong Man

However, do not rejoice that the spirits submit to you, but rejoice that your names are written in heaven.

LUKE 10:20

As there an area of your life where you are spiritually bound? Is there something that you desperately wish you could break out of, but you feel powerless to do so?

At the beginning of His ministry, Jesus proclaimed that He had come to fulfill what the prophet Isaiah wrote: "The Spirit of the Sovereign LORD is on me, because the LORD has anointed me to preach good news to the poor. He has sent me to bind up the broken-hearted, to proclaim freedom for the captives and release from darkness for the prisoners" (Isaiah 61:1). Jesus came to release us from Satan's hold.

But Jesus never sugarcoated His message. He drew the line, putting God on one side, Satan on the other. Then He tells us to "bind the strong man." To rephrase, "Don't let Satan have an inch."

Don't settle for less than God's best. Bind the strong man and let God's power and presence take control of that part of you which rightfully belongs to Him.

Tomorrow Can Be Beautiful

Faith and God's Faithfulness

*By faith we understand that the universe was
formed at God's command, so that what is seen
was not made out of what was visible.*

HEBREWS 11:3

It is very easy to take God's faithfulness for granted.
Take a look at your children as you tuck them into
bed at night. Take a lingering look at your home. God's
faithfulness to us should inspire our devotion to Him.

When Napoleon Bonaparte was crossing the Alps in
the dead of winter, an avalanche caught a drummer boy
and swept him into a steep crevasse. Quickly the boy
scrambled to his feet and kept the drums rolling even at
the bottom of the crevasse. Someone said, "Let's stop
and rescue the boy." But the officers responded, "You
know Napoleon's order—the columns cannot stop."
And the long columns of soldiers marched and left the
little drummer boy to his death.

Hardened soldiers wept as the story was later told
around campfires. No doubt many discussed the
wisdom in leaving the drummer boy unaided. But
what impressed the soldiers and makes the story worth
re-telling was the drummer boy and his faithfulness.
Is our faithfulness to God of the same quality?

365 Guidelines for Daily Living

The Gentle Shepherd

I am the good shepherd. The good shepherd lays down his life for the sheep.

JOHN 10:11

"He gathers the lambs in his arms. He carries them in his arms. He gently helps the sheep and their lambs," says Isaiah.

Are you a lost sheep cut off from the care of the Shepherd? The Good Shepherd is searching for you far more than you are for Him. God, at times, uses gentle persuasion to get our attention, and sometimes through difficulty—the pain of a broken relationship, the heartache of rejection. When we realize that the missing ingredient of our lives is a relationship with God, the Shepherd of our souls leads us back home.

That's good news, friend. No matter where you are, how far you have strayed, or how great your pain, the words of Isaiah still hold true: The Shepherd of our souls still lifts the fallen; He restores the wounded; He cares for you.

Tomorrow Begins Today

Healing in the Loving Touch

People were also bringing babies to Jesus to have him touch them.

LUKE 18:15

*H*ave you ever considered the impact of a loving touch? There were times when Jesus healed sickness with a command. But there were other occasions when He reached out and touched someone.

He touched the leper who went through life crying, "Unclean, unclean!" and He still touches those who are neglected by society today.

When asked how she had become involved in her work with the mentally-challenged, a woman named Pungaja, who was handicapped herself, said that missionary Amy Carmichael had changed her life with one hug. "When she hugged me," Pungaja said, "all my burdens went away!"

People respond to loving touch. A family counselor says that most unwanted teenage pregnancies could have been prevented if a father only hugged his teenage daughter everyday.

"Is any sick among you?" wrote James to the church almost 2000 years ago, "let him call for the elders of the church; and let them pray over him, anointing him with oil in the name of the Lord" (James 5:14 *KJV*). There is healing in the touch of love and faith.

Today Can Be the Best Day of Your Life

Empowerment

But you will receive power when the Holy Spirit comes on you.

ACTS 1:8

Simply put, empowerment means that individuals want part of the action. They are tired of being unrecognized, and they want some say in what happens.

Empowerment has a spiritual dimension as well, although the definition of "empowerment" is somewhat different. God's empowerment, which He promised to His children, opens the door to a new dimension of spiritual life for any who is willing to receive it on God's terms, not his own. It's the three words "on God's terms" that cause us trouble.

When people demand empowerment, it is usually on their own terms. But empowerment from God—the real thing—only comes through Jesus Christ. Jesus Himself promised us empowerment right before He went to heaven. He said, "But you will receive power when the Holy Spirit comes on you . . ." (Acts 1:8).

Spiritual empowerment isn't some bells and whistles sort of spiritual jazz to make our drab lives exciting. It is how God chooses to work through us to touch the lives of other people. Empowerment comes when we meet God's terms and ask Him to fill us with Himself.

May God give us a thirst for spiritual empowerment.

Tomorrow Begins Today

Too Much Stress

In this world you will have trouble. But take heart!
I have overcome the world.

JOHN 16:33

Not all stress is bad. Stress causes the tension which holds a suspension bridge over raging waters. Stress on the strings of a violin allows the beautiful melody to come from the fingers of the master as he glides his bow across the strings. But of course, too much stress causes the bridge to collapse and the strings of the violin to snap.

Most people operate better and are far more productive with some stress. The problem is not stress but too much stress.

In the Upper Room discourse Jesus told the disciples, "In this world you will have trouble. But take heart! I have overcome the world" (16:33). The word Jesus used, *thlipsis*, translated "trouble" includes stress. In the world you will have stress, but you don't have to be consumed by it. Coping—not eliminating all stress—is the key to moving from mere survival to significance.

365 Guidelines for Daily Living

When You are Tired and Discouraged

But those who hope in the Lord will renew their strength . . . they will run and not grow weary.

ISAIAH 40:31

Have you ever had one of those days when you were dead tired and discouraged? Do you want to whip the blues the next time you feel this way?

During these times of discouragement, remember the prophet Elijah. His life shows us that even spiritual giants can get tired and discouraged.

Elijah's life shows that there is a definite relationship between the physical, the spiritual, and the emotional. When Elijah became tired and discouraged, he forgot how God had met his needs in the past, how God sent ravens to feed him at Cherith and how God sent him to Zarephath, where he miraculously brought the widow's son back to life.

Do not despair when you are tired and discouraged. We all feel that way at times. David found an answer for such times: "Wait on the LORD: be of good courage and He shall strengthen thine heart: wait, I say, on the LORD" (Psalm 27:14 KJV).

Today Can Be the Best Day of Your Life

Cleansing for All

Cleanse me with the hyssop, and I will be clean;
wash me, and I will be whiter than snow.

PSALM 51:7

No person is perfect that he does not need cleansing and forgiveness. Paul said this about the cleansing by God's Spirit: "Christ loved the church and gave himself up for her to make her holy, cleansing her by the washing with water through the word" (Ephesians 5:25-26). True, we sin against others and must learn to seek forgiveness, but ultimately the issue is between the individual and his Maker.

Psalm 51 is a prayer of David. In it he cried out, "Have mercy on me, O God according to your unfailing love; according to your great compassion blot out my transgressions. Wash away all my iniquity and cleanse me from my sin" (Psalm 51:4). David knew that he had sinned against Bathsheba. He knew he had sinned against Uriah, her husband. But he also recognized that he had sinned against God. He cried out, "Against you [God], you only have I sinned and done what is evil in your sight" (Psalm 51:4).

But there is good news. What David sought is what God dispenses. To find cleansing and forgiveness, you only need ask God for it.

Today Can Be the Best Day of Your Life

When the Bad Guy Gets Promoted

For evildoers will be cut off, but those who wait for the LORD, they will inherit the land.

PSALM 37:9 NASB

Have you ever faced a situation where honesty and hard work only put you further down the ladder? I received a letter from a woman whose husband was promoted to sales manager in his company after seventeen years of hard work. Then, very suddenly and without cause, the man was demoted and made a salesman—the same position he had when he started. "Why does God answer with loss rather than gain? At least, it appears this way," the woman wrote.

GUIDELINE 1: Remember, the Bible stresses the *ultimate*, not always immediate, triumph of right in an evil world.

GUIDELINE 2: Know that evil produces evil. Treat the evil person as he treats you, and you will have succumbed to the very thing you detest.

GUIDELINE 3: Realize that the final test is not who gets the promotion but who gets God's nod of approval.

GUIDELINE 4: Hold on to what you know is right. Rest on the promises of a Sovereign God and wait patiently for the final outcome.

Today Can Be Different

Through the Trials

Be strong and courageous, do not be afraid or tremble at them, for the LORD your God is the one who goes with you. He will not fail you or forsake you.

DEUTERONOMY 31:6 NASB

*T*rials do not mean that God has singled you out for special punishment, or that you're not a victorious Christian. Trials happen, and God promises to be with you when they do.

Here are some observations about the deep waters through which you may pass:

1 Trials never leave you where they find you. Like a whirlwind that picks up an object, when you finally hit the ground you are not in the same place; you're not even the same person.

2 Trials will cause you to grow better or bitter, depending on what you're made of.

3 Trials could produce growth and maturity.

4 Trials are of limited duration. No matter how deep the water, eventually God will lead you to the other side.

5 Trials could lead you to know His presence and power that you otherwise would never experience.

Don't curse your trials; realize God is with you through them. His presence will make a difference.

Today Can Be Different

Lord, Teach Us to Pray

Lord, teach us to pray, as John also taught his disciples.

LUKE 11:1 NKJV

In public, Jesus' prayers were short; in private, long. Our prayers tend to be the opposite—lengthy when we wish to impress people but very short or non-existent in the privacy of our homes or bedrooms. We need to learn to pray to develop the kind of relationship Jesus enjoyed with His Father.

Let's look at the first phrase of the Lord's Prayer, *Our Father*. Notice the possessive pronoun *Our*. At least 75 times Jesus used the term *My*, saying, *"My Father."* But in praying "Our Father," Jesus reminded the disciples that God is the Father of all who have come to peace with His Son through His blood on the Cross.

When we address God as *Our Father* in our prayers, we are in the company of brothers and sisters all over the world.

Notice, too, the selflessness in this term *Our*. Not *I*, not *me*, or *my* . . . but *Our Father*. The Church of Jesus Christ crosses cultures, prejudices, languages, and barriers. No nation in the world is devoid of those who name the name of Jesus Christ and pray to the Almighty as Sovereign Lord and God.

365 Guidelines for Daily Living

Our Father

This, then, is how you should pray: "Our Father in heaven . . . ."

MATTHEW 6:9

When the disciples came to Jesus and asked, "Lord, teach us to pray," Jesus began by saying, "Our Father!" Of all the terms which Jesus could have used —"Almighty God" or "Great Creator" or "Oh Thou, Maker of heaven and earth," He chose simply to use the word "Father"—a word that is warm, intimate and personal.

All prayer is based on a relationship, the relationship of a child with his or her father "Yet to all who received him, to those who believed in his name, he gave the right to become children of God" (John 1:12).

The term "Father" is a term of reliance and of respect. It was the time of the Cuban missile crisis. President John F. Kennedy has just called a press conference in the Oval Office of the White House when a door opened and his four-year-old son wandered into the room. The press conference stopped as a father put aside the lofty affairs of government because his child needed him. This is a picture of our heavenly Father's concern for you. He is never so busy running the world that He doesn't hear or have time for even the most insignificant cry of His children.

365 Guidelines for Daily Living

Where is God's Heaven?

I am going there to prepare a place for you . . .
that you also may be where I am.

JOHN 14:2-3

When the disciples came to Jesus and asked Him to teach them to pray, He said, "This is how you should pray: 'Our Father in heaven . . . .'" Just where is heaven?

Of one thing we are sure, heaven is a real place, the throne room of the Almighty, and from there God rules in the affairs of humankind. The word Jesus used for "place" is the same word which gives us the English word *topographical*. It was always used of a real place, never a figurative, make-believe place.

In many countries, in front of government offices you will find the country's flag proudly flying. The seat of government is in the capital, but wherever you find a government office, you find government representation, and that's how I think of God's people in relationship to heaven.

When you pray those words, "Our Father who art in heaven," remember God is unlimited when it comes to time and space. Therefore, you can be more certain of heaven than you are of anything on earth.

365 Guidelines for Daily Living

Thy Kingdom Come

Going a littler further, he fell with his face to the ground and prayed, "My Father, if it is possible, may this cup be taken from me. Yet not as I will, but as you will."

MATTHEW 26:39

A youth spoke admiringly of his father: "When Dad's in trouble, he always prays." Are you like that child's dad?

When Jesus taught His disciples the Lord's Prayer, the first three points focused on God's rule on earth, and had nothing to do with personal needs—Hallowed or holy be Thy name, Thy kingdom come, and Thy will be done.

When I pray "Thy kingdom come", I am asking God to rule and reign in the affairs of life today. Beyond that, I am asking Him to have His way in my own life personally. Jesus told us that "... the kingdom of God is within you" (Luke 17:21). This means I must let the Sovereign Lord of the Universe reign in my own life personally.

Every child of God must make that decision to let God reign supremely in his life and be the rightful King of his heart. God never forces His will on yours nor overrules your personal will. Yes, indeed, "Thy kingdom come; Thy will be done on earth as it is in heaven."

365 Guidelines for Daily Living

Our Daily Bread

Ask and it will be given to you; seek and you will find; knock and the door will be opened to you.
MATTHEW 7:7

One of the things which Jesus said we should pray for is "our daily bread." To most people today, nothing is more basic to survival than bread or rice. The vast majority of the people in our world are just one meal away from hunger. Thus a plea for daily bread is a cry for sustenance and basic survival.

In teaching this, Jesus made us understand that the basic necessities of life are not a matter of indifference to our heavenly Father. But if God is so concerned, why doesn't He just automatically give us everything we need? Part of the reason is that we may know the answer has come from His hand. Jesus said, "Your Father knows what you need before you ask Him" (Matthew 6:8), yet He also said, "Ask and you will receive and your joy will be complete" (John 16:24).

Begin today with those beautiful words, "Our Father in Heaven" and pour out your heart. It's OK to ask Him for the simple things that you need. That's what prayer is about.

365 Guidelines for Daily Living

A Heart Divided

*Teach me your way, O LORD, and I will walk in
your truth; give me an undivided heart, that I may
fear your name.*

PSALM 86:11

A heart divided is like a kingdom with two kings,
two kings cannot rule the same subjects. Long
ago David prayed that God would teach him His way
and give him an undivided heart (Psalm 86:11).

Let me give three suggestions on how to have an
undivided heart:

1 Decide whom you intend to serve and run up the
flag. A person torn between the world and allegiance
to Christ is miserable. He enjoys neither.

2 Close the door on what divides your loyalty.
Leaving the door open to satiate your old sinful nature
only plants the seeds of failure. Close the door on the
past, so there is but one direction to go.

3 Get involved. Far too many people choose to
follow the Lord without getting involved in His cause.
The body of Christ is a fellowship of believers who need
each other. Get involved in a men's or women's group.
Be part of a church. Get into a support group. Share
your heart, and discover that there are others who have
faced the same issues that have divided your heart.

Today Can Be the Best Day of Your Life

Living Sacrifices

Therefore, I urge you, brothers, in view of God's mercy, to offer your bodies as living sacrifices, holy and pleasing unto God—this is your spiritual act of worship.

ROMANS 12:1

The Apostle Paul was persuaded that there is but one God, the living God, who had made human bodies His temples indwelt by the living Spirit of God Himself. In light of this, Paul's concept of the body as a "living sacrifice" was revolutionary!

Paul says we as believers today should give ourselves —alive, vibrant and joyful—for His cause. He calls this our "reasonable service." Jesus said, "If anyone would come after me, he must deny himself and take up his cross daily and follow me" (Luke 9:23).

In Paul's letter, he followed by giving the key to this whole issue. He wrote, "Do not conform any longer to the pattern of this world, but be transformed by the renewing of your mind" (Romans 12:2). What we need today is the kind of radical commitment that says, "Yes, I will follow Jesus! I'm His—body, soul and spirit!" If this is true of us, "Then," Paul says, "you will be able to test and approve what God's will is, his good, pleasing and perfect will" (Romans 12:2).

Today Can Be the Best Day of Your Life

Joy

The joy of the LORD is your strength.

NEHEMIAH 8:10

"Joy," wrote G. K. Chesterton, "is the gigantic secret of the Christian." Yet for many Christians joy seems to be a well-kept secret that they never really discover it at all.

Joy is distinctly a Christian virtue stemming from new life within—life that has its source in God. Unlike happiness, which often depends on circumstances, joy endures even when circumstances are dismal. Jesus said, "These things I have spoken to you that My joy may be in you, and that your joy may be made full" (John 15:11 *NKJV*).

Would you like to discover joy? Then let God's Holy Spirit begin to fill your heart and life, for real joy comes as the fruit of the Spirit (see Galatians 5:22) and as the result of His indwelling presence (see Romans 14:17). The Apostle Paul further writes, "Now may the God of hope fill you with all joy and peace in believing, that you may abound in hope by the power of the Holy Spirit" (Romans 15:13 *NKJV*).

As author Eugene Kennedy says, "The headwaters of joy are in the heart."

Today Can Be Different

I Can't Help the Way I Am

Why are you downcast, O my soul? Why so disturbed within me? Put your hope in God, for I will yet praise him, my Savior and my God.

PSALM 42:11

Depression is like a torpedo which can cause us to gradually sink into the sea of despair. But much of our depression is the result of situations that can be changed. Depression is often created by circumstances that we have grudgingly come to believe and eventually accept. It is when we accept a bad situation as being permanent that depression, like fog on a winter's day, begins to creep in.

How do you break out of depression? Falling back on an excuse doesn't change the situation. Understanding that staying depressed is sometimes a choice—a very poor choice that you have made that can be reversed —is the first step in turning your life around.

Have you ever been tempted to say, "No wonder I'm the way I am. Look at what happened to me"? If so, say, "I can't help what happened, but I can help what happens from this point on," and by the grace of God, begin to turn depression into victory. Never let depression be a choice that you make by default.

Today Can Be the Best Day of Your Life

Breaking the Bondage of Depression

From the end of the earth will I cry unto thee, when my heart is overwhelmed lead me to the rock that is higher than I.

PSALM 61:1-2 KJV

*M*ost of the time, our problems in life result from our inability to see a way out of bad situations that have gradually taken us captive.

Do you want to reverse a bad situation that is depressing you? If so, follow the following guidelines:

1 Realize that depression is a choice that you have made, a bad choice that can be reversed.

2 Understand that what happens to you is of concern to God. There is forgiveness for your failure and hope for your despair. There is a God who cares for you.

3 Refuse to accept the thought that your depressing circumstances are permanent. Turn your problem into a stepping-stone that leads to victory.

4 Understand that while people can help, they can't do everything for you. You and God have to form a partnership in this process of turning your life around. Depend on God—you will find that He is enough.

Today Can Be the Best Day of Your Life

Stress and Pressure

Listen to my cry for help, my King and my God,
for to you I pray.

PSALM 5:2

What do a businessman in New York, a secretary in Hong Kong and a tribal leader in a mountainous area of the Philippines have in common? Believe it or not, it is tension.

Yes, even in the remote corners of the world, tension and stress are on the increase. So whether you chew betel nuts or the end of a pencil, you live in a world of unrelenting pressure.

Now, not all pressure is evil. Pressure forms the diamond and keeps the tires of a car inflated. But we need to realize that much of our stress and strain today is the result of our living lives that are far busier than God ever intended them to be. Just as too much pressure burns up the diamond and blows out the tires, so will too much pressure ruin you. Balance is essential.

Do you want to keep your life in balance? Then learn to include a time of quiet rest and spend time with God each day. In prayer, look to Him for guidance and direction for the stress you face today.

Today Can Be Different

Thought-Driven Worship

God is spirit, and his worshipers must worship in spirit and in truth.

JOHN 4:24

In his book *The Heart of Praise*, Jack Hayford has a chapter entitled, "Come Before His Presence With Thinking, Too!" He says that God is a great God, but to understand how great He really is requires thought.

Thought-driven worship goes beyond worship that is emotionally driven. It is never put on the basis of "I feel like praising the Lord," or "I'm feeling good today, so I guess I will go to church." This is not to suggest that your emotions do not respond to the greatness of God—they do! The indwelling presence of the Almighty brings love, joy and a spectrum of wholeness that touches every aspect of your being.

Thought-driven worship takes into account what God has done and responds from the person's whole being. Think of these words: "Many, O LORD my God, are the wonders you have done. The things you planned for us no one can recount to you; were I to speak and tell of them, they would be too many to declare . . . But may all who seek you rejoice and be glad in you . . ." (Psalm 40:5, 16).

Today Can Be the Best Day of Your Life

Being Thankful

Give thanks to the LORD, for he is good; his love endures forever. Let the redeemed of the LORD say this . . .

PSALM 107:1-2

Historian Will Durant observed that one of the indications that decay is prevalent in a society is the inability to express personal gratitude and appreciation.

Some folks go through life complaining, pointing out how difficult things are. They are envious of the person who lives better, wears nicer clothes, and seems to get the good breaks. Have you learned that the attitude of gratitude is a habit that must be cultivated?

For what should you be thankful? Take time to sit down and make a list. But gratitude should never be measured on the basis of how large is the pile of things you have accumulated. It grows out of the realization that the Almighty has blessed you. "Oh that men would praise the LORD for his goodness, for his wonderful works to the children of men!" (Psalm 107:8 KJV) Is that the refrain of your heart in good times as well as hard times? Being thankful is an attitude that brings wholeness and health to our souls.

365 Guidelines for Daily Living

How Big is God? (1)

Great is the LORD and most worthy of praise;
his greatness no one can fathom.

PSALM 145:3

*H*ow big is God? Ask ten people today, and you are apt to get at least ten different answers.

How big is God? He is bigger than your financial need. He is bigger than the problems that confront your business or marriage. Bigger than the conflict that divides individuals and groups, and even nations.

How big is God? Certainly He is bigger than the greatest need of your heart. God still says, "Come now, and let us reason together, saith the LORD; though your sins be as scarlet they shall be as white as snow; though they be red like crimson, they shall be as wool" (Isaiah 1:18 KJV).

God is greater than anything you can imagine; He is limited only by your refusal to let Him work in your life. He invites you to come to Him but He never forces His will upon you.

"Come to me, all you who are weary and burdened, and I will give you rest" (Matthew 11:28). Jesus invites you to discover His true greatness.

365 Guidelines for Daily Living

How Big is God? (2)

But the plans of the LORD stand firm forever,
the purposes of his heart through all generations.
PSALM 33:11

Go out on a dark night and look at the stars. What you see is only a tiny fraction of what is out there. Billions of stars make up our galaxy, yet astronomers say that there are over 500 million galaxies in our universe. An astronomer at Harvard University showed a visitor a photographic plate, 8 x 10 inches, and told him that it showed an area containing 80,000 stars, yet covered a space in the heavens no larger than the visible moon.

Since God created the heavens and the earth as the Bible declares, then surely He has to be bigger than all of His creation.

Do you believe God is bigger than the problem that kept you awake last night, restlessly tossing and turning? Do you believe that God is bigger than the rebellion of your son or daughter? Then why not turn to Him and ask His help?

How tragic to worry as though we have no God. God is bigger than any situation you cannot handle.

365 Guidelines for Daily Living

September

It was you who set all
the boundaries of the earth;
you made both summer and winter.

PSALM 74:17

Looking Back

I press on toward the goal to win the prize for which God has called me heavenward in Christ Jesus.

PHILIPPIANS 3:14

Dwelling on past mistakes and failures is like trying to drive by looking in the rearview mirror. You may be focused, but your field of vision is limited. You're apt to back over curbs or plow into objects you had no idea were there.

Get rid of the rearview mirror in your life once and for all. How? That's where the grace of God's forgiveness comes into the picture. The Apostle Paul bore a load of guilt so great that he would have been a candidate for a mental institution had he not learned that when God forgives, He forgets. We need to learn the same lesson. God made Christ bear our sin so that we might be made righteous in the sight of God.

Would God lie? Never! Then why not accept what He says about your life and get on with it? Forget the rearview mirror and focus on the road that lies ahead.

Tomorrow Begins Today

Standing Up When You Stumble

And mark out a straight, smooth path for your feet so that those who follow you, though weak and lame, will not fall and hurt themselves, but become strong.

HEBREWS 12:13 TLB

Anyone who had watched the 400-meter semifinals in the 1992 Olympics will never forget it. During the race, Derek Redmond, a British runner, tore a hamstring and collapsed on the track. For a few seconds, he lay there on the track, then slowly got to his feet and began dragging himself painfully toward the finish line.

Derek's father, thinking that his son was trying to get off the track, came out of the stands, ran to the track, and put his arm around his son. But Derek wasn't about to quit the race, even though he could not win. Instead, with his dad supporting him, he slowly began to hobble toward the finish line. The crowd, sensing what was happening, began to cheer.

God doesn't prevent the torn hamstrings of life, but He loves us enough to support us in our pain and problems. When you are felled by something in life, you'll discover that the strong arms of your heavenly Father will support you and keep you going.

Tomorrow Can Be Beautiful

Faith—What It Is

Now faith is the assurance of things hoped for,
the conviction of things not seen.

HEBREWS 11:1 NASB

*W*ords mean different things to different people. How do you explain faith in God? Charles Spurgeon once said, "You may think that it is very easy to explain faith, and so it is; but it is easier still to confuse people with your definition."

Do you disbelieve everything you have not seen with your own two eyes? Have you ever seen a neutron or a proton? Of course not, yet electricity is made of these smaller-than-microscopic particles. Science in recent years has produced all kinds of evidence for the reality of unseen objects. Would you call that faith? Again, have you ever seen a note of music? No, but you have heard one. Whose heart does not thrill to the beautiful song of a bird or the lilting strains of an orchestra?

Faith in God is based upon certain empirical facts: As God has done in the past, He will meet your needs in the present.

If faith in God is only academic to you, go to the source itself. Remember, faith comes by hearing, and hearing by reading the Bible.

365 Guidelines for Daily Living

The Testing of Your Faith

Anyone who comes to him must believe that he exists and that he rewards those who earnestly seek him.

HEBREWS 11:6

George Müller spent most of his life in Christian work but he never asked anyone for money—not once. His secret was faith in God. He relied on God for the means of feeding and clothing more than 10,000 orphans in Bristol, England.

Müller wrote, "Faith is the assurance that the thing which God has said in His word is true, and that God will act according to what He has said in His word. This assurance, this reliance on God's Word, this confidence, is faith."

During periods of testing, faith is holding on to what we know is true. We won't understand everything, but if we keep on trusting God, we will eventually see the working of His hand. And when you see His hand it becomes easier to trust His heart.

With God's demand for simple obedience comes His promise to provide and protect. For George Müller, it was trusting God to provide for the orphans of Bristol. For you, it may be trusting God for the strength to get through another day. The good news is that God is the same "yesterday and today and forever."

Tomorrow Begins Today

The Sovereign of the Universe

And Joshua said, "Ah, Sovereign LORD, . . . if only we had been content to stay on the other side of the Jordan!"

JOSHUA 7:7

God's sovereignty creates binding consequences for our relationship with Him. If He is sovereign, then I am His subject. If He is fully in control, then what I think about Him is not nearly as important as what He thinks about me.

Many people prefer not to think about God's sovereignty, or consider their relationship to Him. For those who have never learned about God's nature—His mercy, kindness, grace, and goodness—the thought that God is absolutely in control is rather frightening. The real issue separating mankind from the grand and comforting truth of God's sovereignty is that we are fearful of losing control.

Understanding the nature and character of God is the key to knowing Him. When you really know Him, you will love Him; and when you love Him, your fears will disappear.

Tomorrow Can Be Beautiful

Praying When Life Unravels

Whatever you ask for in prayer, believe that you have received it, and it will be yours.

MARK 11:24

How do you pray when your world is falling apart? Do you stop praying and conclude that God has ignored you? Many people give up on God because they prayed for something and it didn't happen.

In his book *Too Busy Not to Pray*, Bill Hybels explains why some prayers are unanswered. He says, "If the request is wrong, God says, 'No.' If the timing is wrong, God says, 'Slow.' If you are wrong, God says, 'Grow,' but if the request is right, the timing is right and you are right, God says, 'Go!'"

Simply put, God answers us in four ways:

1 Some answers are direct. We ask and immediately receive what we've asked for.

2 Some answers are delayed. God answers us on His timetable, not ours.

3 Some answers are disguised. We ask for something and later we recognize that God answered differently from our request—but His answer was much better.

4 Some answers are denied. God loves you too much to give you everything you ask for. Father does know best, and you can trust God for the best in your life.

Today Can Be the Best Day of Your Life

The Burden of Understanding

Jesus said to him, "If I will that he remain till I come, what is that to you? You follow Me."

JOHN 21:22 NKJV

The question "Why?" echoes down through the centuries. But God never gave us the burden of understanding. What He gave us is the responsibility of obedience.

If you want answers to the issues you struggle with, start by studying the Bible seriously. It's the only Book that answers the tough questions of life: "Who am I? Where did I come from? Why am I here? Where do I go five minutes after I die?" Only God can give purpose to living in an imperfect, confusing world.

You have a choice: You can go through life making excuses for yourself because "this is not fair" or "that is not right," or you can focus on a single issue: "What does God want me to do?" Obedience brings God into your life and adds a third dimension. "Understanding why" is something you have to leave with God, believing that He is a God who loves you and cares about your life and that He is faithful.

Don't make life too hard by trying to understand what only God can fathom.

Tomorrow Can Be Beautiful

Be Still

Be still and know that I am God.

PSALM 46:10 KJV

Do you find yourself so caught up in the rush of 21st Century living that you can scarcely remember what day it is? You jump out of bed, gulp down your coffee, hurry to work, then rush home and eat dinner in record time to make your evening appointment. Then it's off to bed so you can do the same things all over again the next day.

Be still—so you can hear God's voice. Times of quietness are part of His natural laws. God has not promised to spare us from difficulty. We ask to be lifted above our cares, and He sends sorrows. We ask for light to see the path ahead, but clouds appear. We ask for peace and quiet that we may meditate, and everything around us swirls in confusion. Sometimes God allows trials because He knows these things will drive us to Himself and teach us that when He gives peace, no one can make trouble.

When we are weak, God does not say be *strong* but be *still.* "In quietness and confidence shall be your strength" (Isaiah 30:15).

Today Can Be Different

Trust His Heart

In him we were also chosen, having been predestined according to the plan of him who works out everything in conformity with the purpose of his will.

EPHESIANS 1:11

How do you know whether it is God, the devil, or just circumstances that is behind the things that happen?

Following the death of his sweet wife of thirty-three years, Vance Havner wrote, "Sometimes when trouble hits you real hard, it is tough to determine whether it is divine chastisement or a devilish attack." The months when she lay dying were the darkest days of his life. He says, "For me this meant five months by a hospital bed of a dying wife who was wasting away with a disease I had never heard of."

Then Havner says, "I do not understand some of the things we went through. There were a lot of things I do not have any clever answer for."

Many times we do not have all the answers to why things happen. Nonetheless, we must continue to walk by faith. Instead of looking for explanations, we can pause and listen to the Father's voice saying, "Trust Me." If you are His child, God works all things after the fashion of His will (Ephesians 1:11).

365 Guidelines for Daily Living

Worry

Peace I leave with you: My peace I give to you;
not as the world gives, do I give to you. Do not let
your hearts be troubled and do not be afraid.

JOHN 14:27

Former U.S. President Lyndon Johnson shares a formula given to him by an old woman. She said, "When I works, I works hard. When I rests, I hangs loose. When I worries, I sleeps."

We worry an awful lot about things that we can neither control nor should greatly be concerned with. "Worry," said George Lyons, "is the interest paid by those who borrow trouble."

But there is a sovereign God who directs the affairs of His children. Instead of worrying, we can put our faith into practice, praying, "God, please take control of my life." God is big enough and gracious enough to keep us from the tragic consequences of our own failures. He can redeem even our mistakes.

Today Can Be Different

On Giving Thanks

Give thanks in all circumstances.

1 THESSALONIANS 5:18

*G*ive thanks? How can we give thanks? All over the world, there are wars, hunger, oppression and unrest. How can we truly give thanks considering the present turmoil?

The prophet Habakkuk also lived during a time of great turmoil. There appeared to be no hope for Habakkuk's nation of Israel. Corruption and confusion were everywhere. "Why does God not intervene?" he asked. "Why is God silent in times of disaster?"

Habakkuk had questions; but he brought them to God. And God not only answered His questions, but He also put a song in Habakkuk's heart. Habakkuk found an answer—God is still on the throne of the universe. He is, from everlasting to everlasting.

You too will find that as you put your faith in Jesus, peace and joy will flood your heart in spite of difficult circumstances. Praise will spring from your heart because your happiness does not depend upon world conditions or material gain, but upon a loving Heavenly Father who is in control and who cares for each one of us.

Today Can Be the Best Day of Your Life

Commitment

Don't you see that you can't live however you please, squandering what God paid such a high price for? The physical part of you is not some piece of property belonging to the spiritual part of you.

1 CORINTHIANS 6:19, TM

*A*fter a revival meeting, a farmer decided to give a marshy section of his farm to the Lord. Later, coal was discovered on it, increasing its value tenfold. The farmer struggled at first yet said, "God, I gave You the land. I guess You own the coal as well."

The next year he noticed a layer of slime on the Lord's parcel. The slime turned out to be oil. Now the property was worth more. Surely the farmer was entitled to some of this windfall. But he confessed, "Lord, I gave You the land and the coal. I'm giving You the oil as well."

Almost every person who says, "I'm Yours, Lord," faces this issue in one form or another. When Paul wrote to the Corinthians he said, "Do you not know that your body is a temple of the Holy Spirit? You are not your own" (1 Corinthians 6:19). If you're a Christian, God has a prior claim on your life.

When you acknowledge that everything God has given you—talents and treasure—belong to Him and you give them to Him, it's amazing what can happen.

Tomorrow Can Be Beautiful

Do You Really Love Me?

Why do you call Me, "Lord, Lord," and do not do what I say?

LUKE 6:46

*O*ne of the weaknesses in popular Christianity today is the overemphasis on God's love and an underemphasis on obedience. Love and obedience are not antithetical to each other. On the contrary, obedience is the result of unconditional love.

Obedience is not a choice; it is not an option that one may select out of several possibilities or lifestyles. Either you are obedient or you are disobedient. Either a man is faithful to his wife or he is unfaithful. Either you walk in obedience to what God expects and requires or your love is less than genuine and sincere.

"Why do you call me, 'Lord, Lord,' and do not do what I say?" Jesus asked those who came for the bread and fish. Don't expect the thrill of a religious experience and a good time without cost (see Luke 6:46).

Jesus' question to Peter, "Do you love me?" is one that you can answer only by measuring your obedience to what He asks of you (see John 21:17). Listen to the quiet echo of that question which never goes away, "Do you love Me? Then keep My commandments."

Tomorrow Begins Today

Waiting

The LORD is good unto them that wait for him,
to the soul that seeketh him. It is good that a
man should both hope and quietly wait for the
salvation of the LORD.

LAMENTATIONS 3:25–26 KJV

*W*e are easily convinced that doing anything is better than doing nothing. Waiting seems to be contrary to progress.

Waiting, however, is not doing nothing. It is a kind of action that prepares us for the right choice in the future. It means finding God's timing and avoiding tragic mistakes. "There is an appointed time for everything," wrote Solomon in the book of Ecclesiastes. Waiting is never easy, but as Martin Luther wrote, "He who waits on God wastes no time."

When God's people were overthrown by the forces of Babylon, many thought that God had forsaken them. Yet God said, "I know the plans I have for you . . . plans to prosper you and not to harm you, plans to give you hope and a future" (Jeremiah 29:11).

God has a plan for you too. Waiting for God is not wasted time. Rather, it will bring your restless heart into conformity with the Divine and prepares you for what He has ahead.

What's your hurry?

365 Guidelines for Daily Living

Breaking the Bondage of Your Old Nature

The law of the Spirit of life set me free from the law of sin and death.

ROMANS 8:2

Have you ever been torn between what you know is right and what you really want to do? Even the Apostle Paul experienced the conflict, admitting, "When I want to do good, I don't; and when I try not to do wrong, I do it anyway" (Romans 7:19 TLB).

If you are fighting the battle of the two natures, take to heart the following three guidelines:

GUIDELINE 1: Keep your relationship with the Lord warm and personal. Read God's Word, and spend time in prayer.

GUIDELINE 2: Keep the right company. Take time to fellowship with other Christians. If you are involved in a wrong relationship, break it off, once and for all. Don't try to justify it.

GUIDELINE 3: Form the right habits. The chains of habit are too weak to be felt until they are too strong to be broken. Replace wrong habits with right ones.

God is still in the business of breaking our bondage and setting us free through the power of His Spirit. That's the real answer.

Tomorrow Begins Today

When You are Frustrated

*How much better it is to get wisdom than gold!
And to get understanding is to be chosen above
silver.*

PROVERBS 16:16 NASB

Did you ever think that spiritual giants never get frustrated? Take Daniel, for instance. Don't you think he was frustrated when he ended up in the lion's den? The devil must have said, "See, buddy, what serving God gets you into?"

One of the natural responses to frustration is anger. Yet anger is seldom the right solution to frustration for it always takes its toll on relationships.

Another response is flight—you can quit. You can just walk right out. Essentially that's what Jonah did when God told him to go to Nineveh with His message. Jonah didn't want to go. His frustration turned to anger. He couldn't fight God so he ran away.

When we're frustrated, we tend to think that we're on our own, that God is either disinterested or too busy to care. That's not true. Jesus Christ lived in a world of frustration. His disciples walked out and left Him in His hour of greatest need. He does know and He cares. That's good news!

Today Can Be Different

How to be an Encourager

Therefore encourage one another and build each other up, just as in fact you are doing.

1 THESSALONIANS 5:11

ncouragement," says Doug Fields, "is a constant yes in a world that says no." Are you interested in being an encourager? There are roadblocks to be dealt with like the following:

1 Insecurity has to be overcome before you can be an encourager. Make a statement of encouragement that is positive, straightforward and without judgment.

2 Inability must be dealt with. If you grew up in a home where nobody ever complimented anybody, as an adult, you will tend to do the same thing. Encouragement is a decision, a choice that you make.

3 Ignorance has to go. Your encouragement may well be the difference between success and failure in the life of your spouse or friend. If you want to be an encourager, begin noticing what people do well, and tell them.

4 Selfishness must be overcome. Ego attempts to build yourself up by tearing down someone else, but encouragement builds the other up, which shows true greatness in your life.

5 Apathy needs to be confronted. The time to encourage someone is now.

Today Can Be the Best Day of Your Life

Build 'Em Up in a World that Tears 'Em Down

May the God who gives you endurance and encouragement give you a spirit of unity among yourselves as you follow Christ Jesus.

ROMANS 15:5

Everybody needs encouragement.

You can develop the art of encouragement by practicing the following:

1 Focus on a positive aspect of a person, and say it. Your comments should focus upon something positive, leave out negative observations. Mixed messages like, "Your sales were pretty good this month, but if you had taken my advice, they would have been better," don't qualify as encouragement.

2 Be sincere in what you say. Encouragement is not flattery; it is a decision to say something good that is true. A phone call, a note, a few words in passing—these do a lot to boost others in a world that puts people down.

3 Cultivate encouragement as a habit. One of the reasons we give so little of encouragement is that our old nature tends to make us look for the flaws and failures of others. In building each other up, we build up ourselves as well.

Today Can Be the Best Day of Your Life

God Can be Known

O God, you are my God, earnestly I seek you;
my soul thirsts for you, my body longs for you,
in a dry and weary land where there is no water.

PSALM 63:1

One paradox of the Christian faith is that God is so different from us, yet He is interested in us.

The differences are obvious. God never grows weary or becomes discouraged. He never worries about today's news or tomorrow's what-ifs. Although God is so much greater than we are, He is knowable.

Some do not know Him because they do not search for Him for the same reason that a thief doesn't look for a policeman—they don't want to be called to account for their actions. Others do not really know God because they are more interested in the pursuit of truth than in Truth itself. Paul Little, the late director of InterVarsity, wrote, "I am disturbed by an attitude that I sometimes discover among Christians as well as non-Christians: the suggestion that the pursuit of truth is all that really counts. People do not really want any answers because that would end their game. For them, the pursuit of truth is everything."

Yet, God is knowable, and the greater one knows God, the greater is one's desire to know Him better. He is the answer to man's searching heart.

Today Can Be Different

Happiness

I have come that they may have life and have it to the full.

JOHN 10:10

How do you find happiness? The truth is, happiness is not dependent on situations but upon your ability to cope with circumstances in life. And for this, you need God's help. He is the One who can give us the power we need to live above our circumstances.

In Romans 8, the Apostle Paul says we can be more than conquerors. He lists some of the circumstances he faced: tribulation, distress, persecution, famine, nakedness, peril and the sword—not the sort of things connected with happiness.

Yet a conqueror is one who knows how it is to go through the heat of battle, to suffer and do without if he has to, so he can win in the end. Because Paul had Jesus Christ in his life, he had the supreme resource he needed to be a conqueror.

If you have been trying to find happiness through your own efforts, may I recommend Christ to you? Jesus said, "I have come that they may have life and have it to the full." Trust in Jesus Christ, and life in its fullest will begin for you.

Today Can Be the Best Day of Your Life

Six Things the Lord Hates

There are six things the LORD hates, seven that are detestable to him.

PROVERBS 6:16

Centuries ago, Solomon reflected on the failure of humanity when he wrote that God hates seven things: "Haughty eyes, a lying tongue, hands that shed innocent blood, a heart that devises wicked schemes, feet that are quick to rush into evil, a false witness who pours out lies and a man who stirs up dissension among brothers" (Proverbs 6:17-19).

What man hates and what God hates are not always the same. We hate to lose; God hates it when men win by dishonesty. We love to be included; God hates it when men are discriminated against and turned away. We bend the truth to make ourselves look good; God hates it when we are dishonest.

God not only hates these seven negative qualities of human behavior, Solomon says they are detestable to Him. Sins such as murder, theft and war don't make the list. The seven deadly sins are flaws of character more than behavior. Why? Every wrongdoing begins with a thought.

Let those seven be a checklist, and examine yourself if your life measures up to God's standard.

365 Guidelines for Daily Living

The Sin of Pride

Pride goes before destruction, a haughty spirit before a fall.

PROVERBS 16:18

No individual makes it to the top on his own. Yet the person whose heart is lifted in pride takes credit for what he or she does not deserve. One of the strange things about this malady is that those who are most infected with it recognize it the least.

Someone has said that pride comes in three forms: pride of race, pride of face, and pride of grace. Pride of race deals with the feeling of genetic superiority, something we are either born with or quickly acquire from our parents and peers. Pride of face deals with arrogance. Pride of grace is the mistaken belief that you are more spiritual than others.

Of one thing we are sure: God hates pride—perhaps more than any other flaw of character. Scripture is right: "Pride goes before destruction, a haughty spirit before a fall" (Proverbs 16:18).

365 Guidelines for Daily Living

Hands that Shed Innocent Blood

When Uriah's wife heard that her husband was dead, she mourned for him. After the time of mourning was over, David had her brought to his house, and she became his wife and bore him a son. But the thing David had done displeased the LORD.

2 SAMUEL 11:26-27

Two of the things God hates as stated in Proverbs 6:16–19 are "hands that shed innocent blood" and "a heart that devises wicked schemes."

Though Solomon did not mention his father's adulterous affair with his mother in this passage, he must have thought of the consequences that followed: the public humiliation, the death of his brother, and the conflicts that split David's family.

But there is forgiveness and healing for our wrongdoing. As the Psalmist wrote, "If you, O LORD, kept a record of sins, O LORD, who could stand? But with you there is forgiveness; therefore you are feared" (Psalm 130:3-4).

If you see yourself in these wrongs which God hates, confess your wrongdoing, forsake it, and find God's strength to overcome your human weakness. This is what grace is about.

365 Guidelines for Daily Living

Loving what God Loves, Hating what God Hates

How good and pleasant it is when brothers live together in unity! It is the precious oil poured on the head, running down on the beard.

PSALM 133:1-2

*L*ong ago, the writer of Proverbs gave us a list of what God loves and what He hates. "There are six things the LORD hates, seven that are detestable to him," wrote Solomon. The seventh in the list is "a man who stirs up dissension among his brothers."

It happens in the office, in clubs, in organizations, and certainly in churches and fellowships: a troublemaker spoils the peace and divides the body through inferences, gossips, and innuendoes.

What God hates is not the person who raises his voice in maintaining purity of doctrine, but the person who maliciously and wrongly divides, usually by what he says. Before you say something be sure that your concern is the same thing that concerns God, not simply an extension of your individual, selfish will. Hating what God hates means we strive for peace and oppose pitting brother against brother.

365 Guidelines for Daily Living

The Inward Man

*But let it be the hidden person of the heart, with
the imperishable quality of a gentle and quiet
spirit, which is precious in the sight of God.*
1 PETER 3:4 NASB

*Y*our voice, your eyes and your dress are three tell-
tale signs about your life, an outward indication
of what you are on the inside.

Your voice, for instance, tells others if you are under
stress or at peace with the world. Your eyes give reveal-
ing signs too. When you are under stress, your pupils
dilate, and you often glance away. Clothes are signs that
tell about you as well. The size of your jewelry or the
intensity of the colors you wear often tells much about
your personality.

What others see when they look at you is important.
But what you are underneath the veneer is far more
important. When people take a good look at you, do
they see sincerity and genuineness? Are you the kind
of a person that causes others to be glad to be with you?
Is there a measure of love, joy and peace, longsuffering,
patience, gentleness and goodness? In short, are you a
person who reflects the presence of God because the
Holy Spirit dwells within you?

May God help us to make our lives as good within
as we want them to appear without.

Today Can Be Different

Responsibility

The person who sins will die. The son will not bear the punishment for the father's iniquity, nor will the father bear the punishment for the son's iniquity.

EZEKIEL 18:20 NASB

Isn't anyone really responsible for anything anymore? A judge's composure would probably be shaken if someone stepped forward and said, "Yes, judge, I did it. I'm responsible, and I accept full responsibility for my actions." But, of course, people who accept responsibility for their actions usually don't end up defending their actions in court.

God says, "The son will not bear the punishment for the father's iniquity, nor will the father bear the punishment for the son's iniquity" (Ezekiel 18:20 NASB). You are responsible for yourself and the consequences of what you do.

While God says you must take responsibility, He also says, "You *can* be different! My grace can change your life." Responsibility and redemption are two sides of the same coin. One side reveals your failure; the other shows you the hope that God will change your life. Life can be different.

365 Guidelines for Daily Living

The Secret of a Happy Life

Be transformed by the renewing of your mind, so that you may prove what the will of God is, that which is good and acceptable and perfect.

ROMANS 12:2 NASB

In her famous classic *The Christian's Secret of a Happy Life*, Hannah Whitall Smith tells of a skeptic who said to her, "You Christians seem to have a religion that makes you miserable. You are like a man with a headache. He does not want to get rid of his head, but it hurts him to keep it. You cannot expect outsiders to seek very earnestly for anything so uncomfortable."

Is God a cosmic kill-joy who has given us a black book full of rules and regulations to keep us out of hell and to take the happiness out of life?

To be a happy Christian is to realize that God can work within us, making our lives the outworking of His Spirit within. We will never be happier than when we are in the center of His will, letting Him work through us to accomplish His purposes.

Are you like the man with a headache? Remember, real happiness comes only by completely doing God's will.

Today Can Be Different

The Clash of Cultures

But as for me and my household, we will serve the LORD.

JOSHUA 24:15

*Y*our family is affected by the culture in which you live and in which your children grow up. At times you can change the backdrop of culture that surrounds your family by moving, but there are other times when you have to live with it. Nonetheless, there are things you can do to either maximize the impact of culture on your lives or to minimize its influence.

By God's grace, your home can be insulation against some aspects of culture, which you feel is wrong and harmful. You have to decide, and then you have to draw the line and say, "Our family is going to be different!"

Paul wrote the Romans, "Don't become so well-adjusted to your culture that you fit into it without even thinking" (Romans 12:2 TM). If you fail to help create the culture that surrounds your family, the world surrounding you will provide that culture.

"But as for me and my household," said Joshua long ago when he was battling the culture of his age, "we will serve the Lord." He did, and so can you and must if yours is to be a godly home and family.

365 Guidelines for Daily Living

Chance of a Nation's Leaders

No one from the east or the west or from the desert can exalt a man. But it is God who judges: He brings one down, he exalts another.

PSALM 75:6–7

What part does chance play when it comes to the establishment and removal of world leaders? Is a man a leader only because of his power and charisma, or does God decree who should lead?

Leadership in our world is not a matter of fate but by the will of the Almighty, who raises one up and humbles another (Psalm 76:6–7).

But what are we to say when a wicked individual comes to power and holds the lives of millions of people in his hands?

When situations develop which bring jeopardy and suffering to humanity, God is working His higher purposes. It is a small matter for God to remove those who blaspheme His Name and refuse to do His will.

Those who walk across the stage of world leadership are there only by the grace of God, who raises up one and humbles another.

365 Guidelines for Daily Living

Saying "Thank You"

Therefore, since we are receiving a kingdom that cannot be shaken, let us be thankful, and so worship God acceptably with reverence and awe.

HEBREWS 12:28

*T*he American poet Carl Sandburg once said, "When a nation goes down . . . [or] a society perishes, one factor will always be true. The people forget where they came from. They lose sight of what brought them this far."

When God's people forgot their heritage and the source of their blessing, they also forgot how to say, "Thank you!" God reprimanded them for their failure. "For you are thankless in addition to all your other faults" was the reproof of the Almighty (see Ezekiel 16:43 TLB).

Have you discovered that gratitude, learning to express appreciation by saying "Thank you," is a habit that must be learned? There's something about our natures that makes gratitude difficult to express, but it is a sign of a man who is at peace with himself and his world who conveys appreciation to those who have helped him.

May God deliver us from the sin of thanklessness.

365 Guidelines for Daily Living

October

All men are like grass,
and all their glory is like
the flowers of the field;
the grass withers and the flowers
fall, but the word of the Lord
stands forever. And this is the
word that was preached to you.

1 PETER 1:24-25

Underneath are the Everlasting Arms

The eternal God is your refuge, and underneath are the everlasting arms.

DEUTERONOMY 33:27

What does "underneath are the everlasting arms" mean? "Underneath means underneath," said George Stormont, a British pastor who was then in his late 80s. No matter how low you are, God will still be there beneath you, to support you and lift you up.

God is underneath your lowest emotions and your darkest night. God will always be underneath your deepest loss. Even underneath your most shameful act, His everlasting arms are there to help you back up on your feet. Whether your most shameful act is something known only between you and God, or it made the front page of the newspaper, God's grace covers the wrong. His forgiveness will make the difference.

The promises of God are not reserved for a handful of saints ready for immediate promotion to heaven. God plays no favorites. Underneath are His everlasting arms. Mark in your Bible that great promise found in Deuteronomy 33. And put your name on it.

Tomorrow Begins Today

A Sovereign God and My Will

I will come and proclaim Your mighty acts,
O Sovereign LORD; I will proclaim Your
righteousness, Yours alone.

PSALM 71:16

hat we choose to believe or disbelieve about God doesn't change who He is. Some create a kind of smorgasbord concept of God, accepting some truths about Him and rejecting those they dislike. But is that any different from fashioning a golden calf as did Israel in the wilderness—making their own God?

Why are you afraid to embrace what the Bible says about God's sovereignty, about His purpose for your life? Fear, right? Are you afraid that God may impose His will on you in a way you won't like?

"God works all things after the counsel of His will," says Paul. God's will for you stems from His loving nature and as an extension of His sovereign plan.

Look up the phrase "O Sovereign LORD" in the Bible and notice the hundreds of times it appears in the prayers of God's people. Then ask yourself, "Why haven't I had my eyes opened to this great truth?" Jesus says: "Then you will know the truth, and the truth will set you free" (John 8:32).

Tomorrow Can Be Beautiful

Which of Us, O Lord, Shall be Sovereign? (1)

O Sovereign LORD, You are God! Your words are trustworthy, and You have given this good promise to Your servant.

2 SAMUEL 7:28

"O Lord, who shall be sovereign—You or me?" I doubt you'll ever hear someone say that in his prayers, but I can tell you that the issue of sovereignty has confronted everyone at some point in his spiritual walk.

Some contend that because God is sovereign, He will do exactly what He pleases, regardless of our prayers. What would happen if a farmer applied the same theology to his crop? Obviously, our Sovereign God sends the harvest, but the farmer toils in harmony with his heavenly Father, praying and working, fulfilling his responsibility to be a good steward.

If you want to align your life with Scripture, then pray as though everything depends on God, and work as though everything depends on you. Prayer will bring your will into harmony with the will of your Sovereign Father. Then you can pray with intensity: "Lord, may Your will be done."

Tomorrow Can Be Beautiful

Which of Us, O Lord, Shall be Sovereign? (2)

Then the LORD will appear over them; His arrow will flash like lightning. The Sovereign LORD will sound the trumpet; He will march in the storms of the south.

ZECHARIAH 9:14

God is sovereign, and what He wills is absolute. If God is sovereign, and I am His child, what are the benefits of knowing that He rules the day?

BENEFIT 1: The responsibility for running the world has been lifted from my shoulders.

BENEFIT 2: Wholeness and peace become my inheritance. I may not understand everything God does, but I can rest in the confidence that He is in control.

BENEFIT 3: God's sovereignty gives me a sense of security both spiritually and emotionally.

BENEFIT 4: God's sovereignty gives me confidence when I pray. He sorts out the dumb things I ask for and only gives me what I really need, because of His great love for me as His child.

Read Romans 8, where Paul so beautifully tells us that nothing can separate us from the love of this sovereign, caring God, neither now nor for all eternity. Yes, thank You, Sovereign Lord.

Tomorrow Can Be Beautiful

Let Us Go On

Christ was sacrificed once to take away the sins of many people; and He will appear a second time, not to bear sin, but to bring salvation to those who are waiting for Him.

HEBREWS 9:28

The writer of the book of Hebrews gives us the following three guidelines for overcoming discouragement and weariness:

GUIDELINE 1: "Let us draw near to God with a sincere heart in full assurance of faith" (Hebrews 10:22). Got troubles, pain, or misunderstanding? Then beat a path to the throne of grace and tell God how you feel.

GUIDELINE 2: "Let us hold unswervingly to the hope we profess, for he who promised is faithful" (Hebrews 10:23). Hold on tenaciously to the promises of God. Don't let anyone talk you out of them.

GUIDELINE 3: "Let us not give up meeting together, as some are in the habit of doing, but let us encourage one another—and all the more as you see the Day approaching" (Hebrews 10:25). When people become isolated from each other, it's like taking a burning piece of wood from the fire: The fire in the wood begins to go out. We need each other for encouragement, for strength, for help.

Study Hebrews 10 and keep on going in life.

Tomorrow Can Be Beautiful

Response to Crisis

When my heart is overwhelmed; Lead me to the rock that is higher than I.

PSALM 61:2 NKJV

People in danger are always an interesting study. Take for instance the evening that violinist Isaac Stern played in a concert in Israel during the Persian Gulf War. In the middle of the concert, sirens began to wail, signaling an attack. Though concertgoers and musicians immediately headed for the nearest exit, Isaac remained calm. He picked up his violin and quieted the audience as he began to play.

How do you respond to crisis? Is there an inner strength that helps you to remain steady in the storm?

It was in a time of crisis that a man cried out, "The LORD is good, a stronghold in the day of trouble. And He knows those who take refuge in Him" (Nahum 1:7 NASB). Nahum lived in a time when the nations of the world were engaged in a deadly conflict. People wondered if God had forsaken them, but Nahum learned to turn to the Lord for strength and help.

Have you experienced this calmness in times of crisis? Go back to the Bible, friend, and learn of God's care and concern.

Today Can Be the Best Day of Your Life

Has God Anything to Say?

This is the way, walk in it.

ISAIAH 30:21

Some think that God has something to say, but that was in the past. Our age today, so they say, is one of scientific advancement and intellectual enlightenment. These people recognize God's existence, but they're not convinced that God really has something to say about our lives today.

God has something to say about our lives today. We just can't hear Him. Amid stress and strain we fail to look to Him for divine guidance and counsel. God has spoken to us through Jesus Christ. In the person of His Son, God says, "I love you and want to have fellowship with you." In His written Word, the Bible, God has provided the guidelines we so desperately need to live purposeful, meaningful lives.

When you follow the directions in God's textbook for living you'll find joy and happiness—not an end in themselves but the product of being rightly related to God through His Son Jesus Christ.

Today Can Be Different

The Cross as a Prism

The people walking in darkness have seen a great light; on those living in the land of the shadow of death a light has dawned.

ISAIAH 9:2

*L*ight in our world falls into three categories— natural light, such as that of the sun, moon and stars; artificial light, which is man-made; and spiritual light. The Bible has a great deal to say about light and what it does to darkness. John, writing the introduction to his gospel, pictures Jesus Christ as the Spiritual Light of the world who came into a world of darkness.

As Sir Isaac Newton discovered, a variety of colors emerges when light passes through a prism, some brilliant and others more subdued. Each color is a particular manifestation of light.

The Cross is the prism through which heaven's light passes and shines on your darkness. No matter what your need is, God is sufficient and able to help. He is the answer to your neediness, the solution to your problem and pain. The Cross reveals to us the Light of the World, who can overcome any darkness that you face. If you find yourself in a dark place right now, look to the Creator of light, who loves you and will give you light for the next step.

365 Guidelines for Daily Living

Be Still and Know

Be still, and know that I am God.

PSALM 46:10 KJV

"Be still and know . . . ." In other words, "Be still—stop your running to and fro—slow down long enough to hear My voice. And know—learn personally and experientially—that I am God." There's so much God would like to reveal to you if only you would slow down long enough to hear His voice.

So many times our relationship with God is need-centered, rather than God-centered. We are so overwhelmed by our earthly desires that all we think of is, "God, I want You to do this for me, and I want it now."

Have we been so consumed with our wants, needs and own little worlds that we fail to explore the depths of God's Word and discover what He is like? Discover in the Bible what God tells us about Himself. Take note of His characteristics and learn to wait quietly on Him. Next, discover what God is like by studying the life of Jesus in one of the first four books of the New Testament.

When you begin to grasp something of His true greatness, you will be truly amazed!

Today Can Be Different

A Thirst for the Almighty

On the last and greatest day of the Feast, Jesus stood and said in a loud voice, "If a man is thirsty, let him come to me and drink."

JOHN 7:37

In the Judean wilderness, David cried out, "O God, You are my God, earnestly I seek you; my soul thirsts for you, my body longs for you, in a dry and weary land where there is no water" (Psalm 63:1). Hunted by Saul, David was tired, maybe wondering if he'd ever be able to go home and sleep without concern for his safety. Yet he did not long for these comforts. No, he cried out that his soul was thirsty for the Lord.

Do you have times in your life when you grow weary of the battle and your soul cries out to God?

To know God intimately, insulate yourself from the noise that keeps you from hearing His voice. We need those quiet, personal, intimate times without telephones and interruptions. Tell God about the deep longing in your heart to know Him and to feel His might and power.

Tomorrow Can Be Beautiful

God Works the Night Shift

God called the light "day" and the darkness He called "night."

GENESIS 1:5

*H*ave you ever worked the night shift? Getting used to the schedule isn't much fun. Everything is different: eating dinner at breakfast time, going to bed when everyone else is getting up, sleeping when others are working or playing. The darkness of the night shift seems to intensify everything. During the night shift, it's quieter, it's lonelier, and it's longer. Sixty minutes at night can seem as long as an entire afternoon with daylight. Not everyone can take the night shift. For most of us, the night shift is too lonely, too dark.

Question: Does God work the night shift?

In his book titled *God Works the Night Shift*, pastor Ron Mehl says that we often hear the voice of God speaking to us in the quietness of the night.

The absence of sunshine is not all that makes for darkness in our lives; it is also the difficulties, the suffering, the results of our stupid mistakes, the losses we sustain. But in the darkness of our lives, we hear God's voice bringing comfort, encouragement, and assurance. Listen for His voice in the darkness. Don't forget: God works the night shift too.

Tomorrow Begins Today

When You Forget that God Works the Night Shift

And David was greatly distressed; for the people spake of stoning him, because the soul of all the people was grieved . . . but David encouraged himself in the LORD his God.

1 SAMUEL 30:6 KJV

One night when worries overwhelmed my sleep, I got out of bed and turned to 1 Samuel 30. I read about the time when David encountered some very difficult circumstances. While David and his men were away from home, the Amalekites kidnapped their wives and children and burned the city. To make matters worse, David's men turned against him.

"But David encouraged himself in the LORD his God," it says in verse 6. David redirected his focus from the darkness of his circumstances to what God had done in the past. He focused on the nature and character of God, not on his own failure. He remembered what we usually forget, that God doesn't abandon us when all trouble breaks loose and the darkness overwhelms us.

Read 1 Samuel 29 and 30, and encourage yourself in the Lord. Remember: He hasn't forgotten you. He hasn't rejected you, He will not fail you, and He gives you the assurance you can turn out the light and sleep.

Tomorrow Begins Today

The Value of Life

Whoever believes in the Son has eternal life, but whoever rejects the Son will not see life.

JOHN 3:36

God views your life as precious. Two thousand years ago God considered you so important that He sent His Son, Jesus Christ, to die for you. He looked at your helplessness and inability to create eternal life, and said, "I'll send My Son to provide eternal life. I'll do for you what you can never do."

What is the worth of the human soul? In God's eyes, it was worth the death of His only Son.

In light of this gift, here is Christ's invitation to you:

> "Come to me, all you who are weary and
> burdened, and I will give you rest."
> Matthew 11:28

May God help you to make faith in Christ your guideline for living. When it comes to life and death, nothing of material value is as important as making sure you have eternal life.

Today Can Be the Best Day of Your Life

Can We See Heaven?

Then I saw a new heaven and a new earth, for the first heaven and the first earth had passed away, and there was no longer any sea.

REVELATION 21:1

The Hubble space telescope, the most powerful telescope man has ever produced, clearly sees objects that are thirty to fifty times fainter than what conventional telescopes can detect. Already the Hubble telescope is letting scientists see things never seen before. A nagging question I have is: On a clear night is it possible for astronomers to focus on heaven itself?

The individual who waits until the Hubble sends back a good picture of heaven may have to wait for a long, long time. Yet heaven is reflected in the face of the person who bends his knees in worship; heaven is mirrored in the servant who washes the feet of his brother.

The scientists who believe in God have wisely focused on heaven. For them it is not necessary to see an image or picture of heaven to accept its reality. They have read the blueprint found in the Bible and are certain that it's there!

365 Guidelines for Daily Living

When You Have Been Disappointed

And hope does not disappoint us because God has poured out his love into our hearts by the Holy Spirit.

ROMANS 5:5

Have you ever had someone let you down?

When you are disappointed in a person, there are several paths you can take. The first is the path that most take: anger and revenge. He hurt you, so you even the score by hurting him back. Seeing somebody else hurt lessens your hurt, so you think.

The second path is withdrawal. You are not interested in taking off his head, but you cannot stand his presence. Therefore, you withdraw and run or stick your head in the sand.

Finally, there is a third path to take—restoration. Do not rejoice when a giant falls. For when he comes down, many weaker, smaller people will be hurt.

When someone you admire proves to be a disappointment, do not step on him nor rejoice in his fall. It takes no great strength of character to see the wrongs of others, but it does take the greatness of grace to forgive and restore.

Today Can Be the Best Day of Your Life

Bless You

Blessed are you when people insult you, persecute you and falsely say all kinds of evil against you because of Me.

MATTHEW 5:11

The English word "happy" comes from the same root word as "happenstance", which means "good luck, chance, or fortune." Good luck, however, is not the same as a blessing from the Lord.

The blessings of God sometimes come as difficulties, or something we would never choose for ourselves. In retrospect we're able to see how God's loving hand gave guidance and direction in such a way that our lives were enriched, strengthened, and broadened.

When you make happiness your goal you will realize that happiness doesn't last. But when you seek blessing from the Almighty, He provides an ongoing source of encouragement. Like a spring that bubbles forth and never dries, God's blessings continue to touch our lives from our birth to our homecoming in heaven.

Don't let the world convince you that happiness is the greatest thing in life. Happiness is a by-product of the Father's blessing; the realization that no matter what the circumstances, God is in charge.

The next time someone casually says, "God bless you!" you can reply, "Ah, yes. I am blessed every day."

Tomorrow Begins Today

Walk, Stand, Sit

Blessed is the man who does not walk in the counsel of the wicked or stand in the way of sinners or sit in the seat of mockers.

PSALM 1:1

Is there anything new under the sun? Emotions that motivate people today are the same as those centuries ago. Greed, sex, lust for power and pride still get people into trouble today.

There is an infinite variety of ways to go wrong and usually only one way to go right. Our mistakes and failures are compounded, but most of the time they stem from one basic mistake—a situation or relationship we knew wasn't good.

Psalm 1:1 says, "Blessed is the man who does not walk in the counsel of the wicked or stand in the way of sinners or sit in the seat of mockers." This describes the progression we often make toward wrong choices.

But the psalmist offers a better way. He says blessed is he whose "delight is in the law of the LORD, and on his law he meditates day and night. He is like a tree planted by streams of water, which yields its fruit in season and whose leaf does not wither" (Psalm 1:2–3).

It's never too late to turn back and realize you missed the right road. It's a decision wise people still make.

Today Can Be the Best Day of Your Life

Hearing the Voice of God

Here I am! I stand at the door and knock. If anyone hears my voice and opens the door, I will go in and eat with him, and he with me.

REVELATION 3:20

Have you ever heard the voice of God within your heart asking you to do something? If you answer "Never!" then is it possible He has been trying to tell you something, and you just haven't been listening or tuned in to His frequency?

How do we recognize the voice of God? Part of the answer comes from the New Testament which tells us "God . . . in these last days has spoken to us in His Son" (Hebrews 1:2).

It's through His Word we most often hear His voice today. I would not be so presumptuous as to tell you that God cannot speak directly to your heart convincing you to do His will. But I can tell you quite clearly that He will never speak anything to your heart that contradicts what He has given to us in His Word.

Do you want to hear His voice more clearly? Take time to read His letters to you in the Bible. Take time to meditate on what you have read, and listen to His voice in prayer.

Today Can Be Different

Let God be God

My times are in your hands.

PSALM 31:15

There are three ways in which God is so different from us that we find it difficult to understand Him. And not understanding Him, we assume that God is the same as we are in these areas.

The first is time. God is never in a hurry. He is not pressed to complete the task by noon on Friday. He knows our tomorrows as well as our todays, and in His own time He does all things well.

God is also different in His unlimited power. Theologians call it "infinitude," which means "limitless." C. S. Lewis once used the illustration of an endless piece of paper upon which you draw a short line to represent your life in relationship to the infinitude of God. A pretty staggering thought, right?

Then too, God's knowledge is complete. Ours is only partial. He sees the end from the beginning, which means that worrying is a waste of emotional energy, when we know our lives are secure in His hands. If you are His, there's no need to fear the future.

Today Can Be Different

Praise

Through Jesus, therefore, let us continually offer to God a sacrifice of praise—the fruit of lips that confess his name.

HEBREWS 13:15

*H*ave you ever had the urge to just break out in song? You may have been inspired by a beautiful morning, or a check that arrived in the mail, or a phone call from a good friend.

As Paul and Silas sat in a Roman prison at Philippi, their feet in stocks, their backs stinging from lashes, they began to sing with joy. To sing in the face of difficult circumstances isn't natural—it's supernatural. When you are in trouble, you want to cry, not sing. Yet in this incident—which took place long ago, there is a great lesson, a guideline for living for us today.

Acts 16 records it for us. Paul didn't feel like singing; yet as a conscious act of the will, he made a decision to lift his voice in a sacrifice of praise. When anyone makes that sacrifice, his spirits are lifted and the joy of the Lord floods his heart. Praise is matter of the will not feelings, and it's the only shortcut to victory.

And that, friend, is what produces joy.

365 Guidelines for Daily Living

Managing Your Fear

Yea, though I walk through the valley of the shadow of death, I will fear no evil: for thou art with me; Thy rod and Thy staff they comfort me.

PSALM 23: 4 KJV

hen Steve Rutenbar was in Ukraine, he went to visit a friend in Kiev who lived on the 12th floor of an apartment building. Since the elevator was not working, he had to walk up twelve flights of poorly lighted stairs.

Steve had only gone a short way when he heard footsteps behind him. Someone was there. Sensing danger and remembering colleagues who had been mugged in similar situations, he quickened his steps. The faster he walked, the faster were the steps of the person behind him. A gentle caring man who stands 6'7" and weighs over 350 pounds, Steve whirled around and crouched in a karate position ready to defend himself. Then he saw the person coming up the stairs behind him—a little girl about twelve years of age.

That's the way with most of our fears. They stalk us and loom much larger in our thinking. When fear seems to stalk you, don't turn and run. Confront it, challenge it, and contain it with God's help.

365 Guidelines for Daily Living

God is Never Late

As the heavens are higher than the earth, so are my ways higher than your ways and my thoughts than your thoughts.

ISAIAH 55:9

God is precisely on time. His timing, however, is different from ours. He is bound neither by time nor space.

Have you learned that it is impossible to fully understand God's timing in our lives? D. Martin Lloyd-Jones wrote: "He may sometimes do the opposite of what we anticipate. . . . Yet it is a fundamental principle in the life and walk of faith that we must always be prepared for the unexpected when we are dealing with God."

God looks at life from a different perspective. He's the timekeeper, and when we think He is late, He's apt to show up, and then we learn our time is in His hands.

When it looked like Jesus was late in arriving, He showed up and raised His friend Lazarus from the dead. God is neither early nor late, He's exactly on time!

365 Guidelines for Daily Living

Reconciliation

But God demonstrates his own love for us in this:
While we were still sinners, Christ died for us.
ROMANS 5:8

In his letter to the Romans, Paul gives us a picture of our reconciliation with God. He points out that God showed how much He loved us by dying for us while we were still sinners.

Having established the Cross as the basis of forgiveness, Paul says, "Since we have now been justified by his blood, how much more shall we be saved from God's wrath through him! For if, when we were God's enemies, we were reconciled to him through the death of his Son, how much more, having been reconciled, shall we be saved through his life!" (Romans 5:9-10).

That is what caused Christ to come! Man had ignored God's direction, and sin separated him from the Father. But God through Christ came to meet us at the point of our disobedience and brought us back into fellowship with the Father.

Have you received the gift that enables you to find God's forgiveness and be reconciled to the Father? God's plan is for you to be reconciled to Him today. Come to the Father through the Son.

Today Can Be the Best Day of Your Life

Don't Worry, Be Happy

But the fruit of the Spirit is love, joy, peace,
patience, kindness, goodness, faithfulness,
gentleness, and self-control.

GALATIANS 5:22-23

"Don't worry. Be happy!" says the lyrics of a song—and why not? Doesn't everyone want happiness?

Happiness in life is conditional and fleeting. It is usually dependent on circumstances, environment, achievement or pleasure. We've placed far too much emphasis on happiness as a right that we deserve.

There is something far more important than happiness; it is joy. Happiness is dependent on circumstances; joy transcends them. You can be joyful even when you aren't happy. Happiness, as the world defines it, involves your environment—your home, your money, your friends and your health. But joy is internal. Happiness is usually temporary; but joy is abiding and remains even when beauty fades. Happiness is material; joy is spiritual. Happiness involves life here and now; joy includes both time and eternity.

The Bible says little about happiness but much about joy. The New Testament writers say that joy is the fruit of the indwelling presence of the Holy Spirit.

Today Can Be the Best Day of Your Life

God Wants You Happy

*For the Jews it was a time of happiness and joy,
gladness and honor.*

ESTHER 8:16

Suppose a reporter from a local newspaper cornered the Apostle Paul after his conversion and asked, "Mr. Paul, how happy are you on a scale of one to ten?"

Paul might look somewhat amazed and say, "Happy? You've got to be kidding." Then, Paul might add, "If happiness were my goal, I'd forget Christianity, buy a villa in the Mediterranean and write books about positive thinking. Now if you're asking about peace and joy amidst the storms of life, that's another matter."

Have you ever thought much about Jesus and happiness? After reading accounts of Jesus' life in the New Testament, do you get the feeling that happiness didn't figure largely in the scheme of what He considered to be important?

Does this mean that God wants us unhappy—that He expects His children to wear black and drink vinegar? Not at all! We're confused today because we think that joy and happiness are synonymous. And using the value system of a godless world, we've put a premium on happiness. Take a few minutes to think about the difference.

Today Can Be the Best Day of Your Life

Happiness that Money Can't Buy

Rejoice in the Lord and be glad, you righteous;
sing, all you who are upright in heart!

PSALM 32:11

Happiness, as most define it, is the world's counterfeit of Christian joy. Joy transcends happiness that is based on possessions and circumstances. But does this mean that godly people cannot be happy or that happy people cannot be spiritual?

Real happiness is a by-product of joy; something that flows like a bubbling spring from the reservoir of joy in the heart. This happiness comes from within. Its source is joy, not material gain.

This was the kind of joy that Jesus had in His ministry on earth, not that which the world seeks. This kind of happiness is not a goal; it is something you discover while doing the will of God in your life.

If you really want happiness, don't search for it. You'll find it as you make God's will your goal in life. The God-dimension brings joy and its by-product, happiness. Only the children of God can fully know or understand this. Joy comes from knowing that God, not circumstances, control your life. This is the only kind of happiness that endures, and this money cannot buy.

Today Can Be the Best Day of Your Life

Thanks for the Many Blessings!

A man's life does not consist in the abundance of his possessions.

LUKE 12:15

From the looks of our bulging closets and garages, we've put a pretty high value on things.

I can't help but recall the words of Russian writer Aleksandr Solzhenitsyn. He said that his life once revolved around things—his books, manuscripts and possessions—until they were taken from him and he was put in prison. He said he never felt stronger than when he realized all his treasures were within himself, and they could never be taken from him.

Friend, take inventory with me for a moment. If fire should strike your home and totally destroy it, would life still be worth living? If your bank account was wiped out, would you feel like committing suicide?

Perhaps you need to pray with me, "Lord, forgive me for the times I've failed to realize that what really is of value in life can never be bought. I'm sorry that at times I've taken for granted my faithful spouse, wonderful kids, and the many friends You've given me. All of them are the result of the blessing of Your hand. Thank You!"

Today Can Be Different

Is There Any Hope?

But Christ was faithful as a Son over His house
whose house—we are, if we hold fast our
confidence and the boast of our hope firm
until the end.

HEBREWS 3:6 NASB

A coalminer was trapped in the mine. His leg was pinned beneath the crushing weight of the timbers and rock that had fallen upon him. For hours he lay in darkness fighting pain and despair, when at last he heard the distant sound of hammers above him and the muffled sound of voices. Unable to call loud enough to make himself heard, he took his pick and in Morse code tapped out the message, "Is there any hope?" Many thoughtful men and women today are asking the same question which the coal miner asked.

Apart from knowing the last chapter of the story of humanity found in the Bible, it seems there is little hope for the world today. But the Bible says that man will not destroy himself by atmospheric corruption. Rather, it offers hope through God's intervention.

God is not only the hope for the future, He's the only hope for the present. Trusting Him gives inner peace—a deep-settled confidence that allows a person to face the realities of life with optimism.

Today Can Be Different

Suicide—a Bad Choice

I am come that they might have life, and that they might have it more abundantly.

JOHN 10:10 KJV

*A*re there situations so desperate that people simply cannot bear them any longer—illness, rejection, pain and depression? Many believe so. They are the sad statistics; people who have given up on life.

Sir Harry Lauder could have been one of them. Lauder, a British comedian, was driven into deep depression when his son was killed. He wrote, "As I faced that crisis, I saw before me three avenues of escape. First, there was alcohol. I could drown my sorrow in alcoholic semi-consciousness. Then, there was suicide. I could seek the oblivion of the grave. And finally there was God. I could seek the comfort of the Eternal. I sought God and found Him."

If you, right now, feel the despair of depression or the pain of life, give someone an opportunity to tell you your life can be different. Pick up the phone and call a pastor or a friend and tell that person exactly how you feel. There is hope. The greatest tragedy of all is for you to give up when life can be different. Life is a decision —one you make everyday. Choose life.

365 Guidelines for Daily Living

What does God Think of Suicide?

Choose life, so that you and your children may live.

DEUTERONOMY 30:19

As a police chaplain, Dick Johnson is often called to assist families of someone who has taken his or her own life. Once, he was called to a house where a suicide had taken place. The body of a young woman lay on a sofa, an unopened Bible on a table only a few inches away from her body. "What a tragedy! There the Bible was, lying on the table with all the answers you would ever need," Johnson said.

For the person who takes his life, suicide has become the solution to an unbearable situation. It is the ultimate and final act of despair.

There is a better way: Trusting God to meet you at the point of your pain and show you out of your difficulty. That plan is found in the pages of His Word, the Bible. Don't leave it lying on the table. Read it today and let it change your life.

365 Guidelines for Daily Living

The Great Commission

For the earth will be filled with the knowledge of the glory of the LORD, as the waters cover the sea.

HABAKKUK 2:14

Long ago Jesus said, "The harvest is plentiful but the workers are few" (Matthew 9:37). Never have those words been truer than today. It has been estimated that more than eight billion people have come into the world since God first created Adam and Eve, and of those, six billion are alive today. This means that more people are alive today than all who have ever died!

The issue is simple: Did Jesus really mean what He said when He challenged the disciples to go into all the world and proclaim the Good News to everyone?

The Great Commission is not an invitation. It is a command given to every follower of Jesus Christ. Years ago God showed me my personal responsibility in helping to reach my generation, and I asked myself, "What is the best means for me to share the Good News?" And that was how *Guidelines* was born.

The Great Commission is still the marching order of those who follow Jesus Christ. How will you fulfill your part?

365 Guidelines for Daily Living

November

ENTER HIS GATES
WITH THANKSGIVING
AND HIS COURTS WITH PRAISE;
GIVE THANKS TO HIM
AND PRAISE HIS NAME.

PSALM 100:4

Hold Everything, It's Bigger Yet

When I consider your heavens, the work of your fingers, the moon and the stars, which you have set in place, what is man that you are mindful of him?

PSALM 8:3

Infinity has multiplied! Based on new calculations, astronomers recently upped their estimate of the number of galaxies from ten billion to fifty billion. This news defies human comprehension.

Until recently, scientists said there were two galaxies for every person on Earth. Now they are telling us that there are ten galaxies for every person alive today. And keep in mind that a single galaxy contains millions, even billions of stars.

The prophet Jeremiah said, "As the host of heaven cannot be numbered, neither the sand of the sea measured: so will I multiply the seed of David my servant" (Jeremiah 33:22 KJV). Psalm 147:4 says that God calls the stars by name and numbers them. Think about it—for every person alive today, there are not just ten stars out there, but ten galaxies.

How awesome God is! He made the universe yet He fills the space of your heart.

Tomorrow Begins Today

When Anxiety Turns to Worry

Don't worry about anything; instead pray about everything; tell God your needs, and don't forget to thank Him for His answers.

PHILIPPIANS 4:6 TLB

One of the reasons we tend to worry is that life can quickly get out of control. When the cause of our concern is a rebellious teenager, an aged parent who depends on us for help, or a family business that seems to be going the wrong way, we can't simply walk away from the situation. Quitting isn't an option.

When anxiety turns to worry, ask yourself the following questions:

• What part of this responsibility is mine, and what must I leave to God to handle?

• Am I turning over to the Lord the part that is His to handle?

• Am I praying with thanksgiving every time I feel anxious?

• Have I focused on the fact that God cares for me?

We have the great privilege of being able to cast our anxiety, our worry, our cares upon God. He is both powerful and loving, and He is in control of what we cannot control. God's sovereignty makes the difference.

Tomorrow Can Be Beautiful

Peace with God

*I, even I, am He who blots out your
transgressions, for My own sake, and
remembers your sins no more.*

ISAIAH 43:25

"Dear Dr. Sala," wrote one young woman, "More than anything else, I would like to know that I have peace with God."

How do you make peace with God?

God sent His Son to make peace with you. The Son walked across a vast no-man's-land—the dark valley between the mortal and the immortal—and was born in Bethlehem. Jesus made it clear that His Father is not an angry enemy who is out to get you.

First, you must understand that God wants you to have peace with Him.

Second step, you must understand that God made Christ bear the punishment of your sin so that you will be accepted, without guilt, in God's sight. Through Christ's death on the cross, God forgave your sins.

Forgiveness, however, isn't automatic. You have to ask for it, confessing your sin. That's your part of the process—the equivalent of running up the white flag and surrendering.

When you know that God has forgiven you, His peace fills your heart.

Tomorrow Begins Today

Jesus, Full of Joy

At that time Jesus, full of joy through the Holy Spirit, said, "I praise You, Father, the Lord of heaven and earth, because you have hidden these things from the wise and learned, and revealed them to little children."

LUKE 10:21

Have you ever experienced reading something in the Bible and suddenly the words leap out at you? Like blinking neon, they cannot be ignored, and you say to yourself, "Funny, I never saw that before."

Recently, as I was reading Luke 10, a phrase leaped from the page and took me captive: "Jesus, full of joy".

I read different translations and all said the same thing. Then I researched on how the word was used elsewhere in the New Testament and in early church writings. I discovered that the word means exactly what the text says. It means "to be glad, to rejoice."

Joy is the by-product of a God-connection which results in the Holy Spirit taking control of our lives. Joy drives back the darkness of circumstances, it goes far beyond the quest for happiness that consumes so many.

If joy is missing in your life, drop to your knees and say, "Lord, I'm short on joy. Please fill my cup." He will.

Tomorrow Can Be Beautiful

The Fear of the Lord

Then the church throughout Judea, Galilee and Samaria . . . was strengthened; and encouraged by the Holy Spirit, it grew in numbers, living in the fear of the Lord.

ACTS 9:31

*M*any people today have lost sight of the consequences of wrongdoing. "It is a dreadful thing to fall into the hands of the living God," says the writer of the book of Hebrews. Yes, God will forgive us, but we cannot escape the consequences of bad behavior.

"Should we then be fearful of God?" I would answer both yes and no. No, in the sense that I love and trust God. To the extent I know how, I've chosen to walk the path of right living. That's what theologians call "a reverential trust." But to be perfectly honest, I'd be mortally afraid to think that I could turn my back on what I know to be true and hope to get away with it. "You may be sure," Moses told the Israelites, "that your sin will find you out" (Numbers 32:23). Those words are just as true today.

The secret is reverential trust. Let your failures drive you to a closer relationship with God because you know you need His help.

Tomorrow Can Be Beautiful

Bitterness

Get rid of all bitterness, rage and anger . . .
Be kind and compassionate to one another,
forgiving each other just as in Christ God
forgive you.

EPHESIANS 4:31-32

*B*itterness, says medical doctor S. I. McMillan, is a killer. It is not the object of the emotion that gets the brunt of the blow; rather, it is the person whose heart is bitter.

Revenge does not eliminate the hurt, but forgiveness does. Yet, forgiveness never comes easy. Jesus set an example when He prayed for His executioners even while He was on the cross, "Father, forgive them for they know not what they do."

Here are some points that may help you to eliminate bitterness and learn forgiveness:

1 To forgive is to follow the example of our Lord.

2 Forgiveness is a necessity in light of the fact that God forgave us.

3 Forgiveness is a matter of the will first, then of the emotions.

4 God helps you learn to forgive as you seek His help.

The four most difficult words to utter in any language are "Forgive me, I'm sorry." Forgiveness is the alternative to the devastation of bitterness.

Today Can Be the Best Day of Your Life

Highest of Human Duties

Encourage him: for he shall cause Israel to inherit it.

DEUTERONOMY 1:38

One of the highest human duties," wrote William Barclay, "is the duty of encouragement. . . . We have a Christian duty to encourage one another. Many a time a word of praise or thanks or appreciation or cheer has kept a man on his feet. Blessed is the man who speaks such a word."

Encouragement to your heart is what oxygen is to your lungs. There are a thousand who tell you when you "blew it," who manage to flash that "I told you so" look when things aren't going well. Yet one person with a word of encouragement can do more to lift you up than the whole lot put together. A word of encouragement can make the difference between success and failure, life and death.

Maybe someone you know is discouraged and feels like quitting. Get in there and encourage him. Maybe you need encouragement too. Anybody can quit; anybody can throw in the towel and walk out. But God believes in you and loves you, and that should be enough to free you to encourage someone else.

Today Can Be Different

Made for God

You will seek me and find me when you seek me with all your heart.

JEREMIAH 29:13

The issue is not whether you can get through life without God—many people do—but how much richer and fuller your life could be with God. You were made by God and for God. As Blaise Pascal described it, within every heart is a God-shaped vacuum which can only be filled by the Almighty. Long ago Augustine acknowledged his need saying, "Thou hast made us for Thyself, O God, and our heart is restless until it finds its rest in Thee."

It is this God-connection which gives meaning and purpose to an otherwise irrational existence. A relationship with God gives certainty that there is an Almighty who is interested in what happens to His children.

Belief in God, however, is not merely a crutch which helps you get through the tough times. It involves a relationship with God which adds a third dimension to all of life. You might feel that you have no need of God if there is no life after death, no heaven or no hell. But if God exists on the other side, you can't afford to live without Him on this side.

365 Guidelines for Daily Living

The Hands of Christ

Look at My hands and my feet. It is I myself!
LUKE 24:39

When mathematics professor Celia Hammond was interviewed by the board of trustees of the university she was applying to, the interviewers politely asked her to remove her gloves and place her hands on the table. Strange request? Not really. The interviewers knew that a person's hands reveal a great deal about his or her life and character.

Have you thought much about the hands of Jesus? His hands are the hands that reached out to the needs of humanity; hands that held little children and blessed them; hands that healed the lame, the blind, the sick; hands that took a little boy's lunch and fed thousands; hands that were nailed to a Roman cross.

The touch of the Master still brings healing, mentally and physically, but most importantly, it brings healing spiritually. When Christ heals a person spiritually, He gives that person the assurance that he or she will live forever. Christ is still in the business of touching lives today.

Today Can Be Different

The Hero of Molokai

All that the Father gives me will come to me, and whoever comes to me I will never drive away.

JOHN 6:37

*F*ather Joseph Damien left his home in Belgium to work among the lepers on the island of Molokai in Hawaii. For twelve years, he tried to share the Gospel to the men and women whose limbs became horribly deformed with leprosy. He achieved little success.

Then Damien reached the end of his patience. Dennis Cone writes, "After twelve long years, he gave up. While standing on the pier about to board the ship that would take him back to Belgium, he looked down at his hands. The white spots he saw could only mean one thing. He had contracted leprosy. So instead of going home, he returned to his work in the leper colony."

As word spread of Father Damien's leprosy among the lepers, hearts melted. Now, he was one of them. He understood their pain, their loneliness, their rejection by society.

Father Damien's story should help you see something of God's care for you. When Jesus came to our planet, He took a step at great personal cost. He experienced our pain our loneliness. And He served to the point of death. He identified with us.

Would you identify yourself with Him also?

365 Guidelines for Daily Living

Hearing God's Voice in the Darkness

He brought me up also out of an horrible pit,
out of the miry clay, and set my feet upon a rock,
and established my goings.

PSALM 40:2 KJV

We no longer take people and throw them into pits, but in ancient days, it was a common practice. The pits we find ourselves in today are more psychological—depression, anger, inadequacy, worry, addiction. Like being in a real pit, it is difficult to be free from them.

David talks about pits more than any other person in the Bible. Emotionally and spiritually, he was in the pits many times.

Sometimes David blamed God for the circumstances that put him in a pit, but David always credited God for delivering him each time. God still delivers from the pit and puts our feet on solid rock.

Do you need help in getting out of the pit? You've tried to get out yourself but failed. Why not ask God's help? There's no need to strike a bargain with God. Just tell Him your need and trust Him completely.

Tomorrow Begins Today

Contentment

Godliness with contentment is great gain.

1 TIMOTHY 6:6

*P*sychologist Joseph Kreisler said, "If you wish to be miserable, think about yourself and what you want. You will spoil everything you touch, and finally you will make pain and misery out of everything God sent you."

Paul would have agreed! He wrote, "Godliness with contentment is great gain." And Paul knew how it is to be content in whatever situation. Paul had been shipwrecked three times. He had been brutally beaten five times and "forty-stripes-save-one." He had walked across most of Asia Minor, traveling hundreds of miles to tell how Jesus Christ transforms lives. Paul had no income or pension, no insurance or endowment, yet, he didn't worry about his next meal, security, position or his future. In fact, he wrote, "I have learned in whatsoever state I am, therewith to be content" (Philippians 4:11 *KJV*).

Contentment can be your portion too, as you learn that God cares for His own. You can be content and happy or miserable and frustrated, as you please. You are the one who decides.

Today Can Be the Best Day of Your Life

The Good Side of Doubt

He will be the sure foundation for your times,
a rich store of salvation and wisdom and knowledge;
the fear of the LORD is the key to this treasure.

ISAIAH 33:6

There is a silver lining to the dark clouds of doubt. A stronger faith results from situations where you need to give honest answers to probing questions. Doubt causes you to dig deep, search for truth, and compare what you have been told with what the Bible says. While some never confront their doubts, others face them and end up better believers because of it.

Even Jesus' disciples felt doubts. Thomas was the foremost skeptic of the twelve who walked with Jesus. He said, "Unless I see the nail marks in his hands and put my finger where the nails were, and put my hand into his side, I will not believe it" (John 20:25).

There are two kinds of doubt: honest doubt and confirmed unbelief—the kind that refuses to accept any evidence. For those who refuse to accept truth, there is little hope; but for the honest doubter, great gain can come. Long ago, God gave a promise: "You will seek me and find me when you seek me with all your heart" (Jeremiah 29:13).

365 Guidelines for Daily Living

Finding an Extra Hour Every Day

Use your heads as you live and work among outsiders. Don't miss a trick. Make the most of every opportunity.

COLOSSIANS 4:5 TM

If you don't determine how to use your time, others will do it for you through their constant interruptions. Without a plan on how to use it, time passes quickly. Take time for what's important. Here are some suggestions:

1 Take time for your spiritual development. I've learned that getting up thirty minutes earlier every day to spend time in the Word and in prayer makes my entire day go better.

2 Take time for what counts—your family. Standing by an open grave, I've heard scores of people say, "If we had only known we had so little time together, we would have . . . ."

3 Take time for yourself. "Dear God," prayed a little boy, "Please take good care of Yourself, because if anything happens to You, we're in big trouble." Take time to guard your health and your relationships.

4 Take time for God. Worship as a family, do His work, reach out to someone who is hurting.

Take time, today.

Tomorrow Begins Today

Staying Cool

A gentle answer turns away wrath, but a harsh word stirs up anger.

PROVERBS 15:1

Does your temper ever get the better of you? How do you stay cool when you are getting hotheaded? The following guidelines may help you:

GUIDELINE 1: Put the issue into perspective. Some things just aren't worth the stress.

GUIDELINE 2: Clear the air. If anger has made chasms between you and your friends, then four words will clear the air: "I'm sorry. Forgive me."

GUIDELINE 3: Deal with problems as they arise. When something bothers you, either deal with it or forget it, but don't hold on to it.

GUIDELINE 4: Begin each day by talking to God about your temper. Admit to Him that you have a problem.

It would be well worth your time to read the book of Proverbs in the Bible and make a careful study of this emotion called anger. It's better when you make temper your servant, not your master.

Today Can Be the Best Day of Your Life

Successful, but Not Very Significant

I tell you the truth, unless a man is born again, he cannot see the kingdom of God.

JOHN 3:3

Nicodemus was successful. He was a member of the Jewish ruling council, which meant that he had influence and prestige. But he also had an empty heart. Searching for an answer to what life was about, he secretly came to Jesus one night.

Unimpressed by Nicodemus's social standing, Jesus cut to the heart of the issue. He told him: "I tell you the truth, unless a man is born again, he cannot see the kingdom of God" (John 3:3). Nicodemus was convicted by what he heard. Later, he defended the actions of Jesus and, when Jesus died, Nicodemus sought to give Jesus a proper burial at no small personal cost to him.

Scores of people today live successful but meaningless lives. Having set out to reach the pinnacle of success in their field, they arrived only to discover that what they thought would bring them happiness only left them disillusioned, empty and frustrated.

How would you define your life—successful or significant? Take time to read John 3 and see if what Jesus told Nicodemus is the solution you need as well.

Today Can Be the Best Day of Your Life

Who is In Charge?

For whom He foreknew, He also predestined to be conformed to the image of His Son.

ROMANS 8:29 NKJV

Of Christ is to be truly Lord of your life, He must have total ownership of it. Having Jesus as the Master of your life relieves you of a tremendous burden. It means that He, who knows the future, is completely dependable and can handle situations that would completely overwhelm you.

Christ as Lord of your life means letting His will be your will. One time we sent the *Guidelines* television crew out on the streets to ask people the question: "Who is in charge of your life?" The replies were: "The government," "My parents," "My husband," "I'm in charge, me!" But only one person replied "Jesus Christ". May I now ask you, "Who is in charge of your life?"

To embrace the lordship of Jesus Christ means that you let Him ascend the throne of your heart! You are the one who needs to say, "Jesus Christ, I want You to be my Lord; please take Your rightful place on the throne of my heart and reign there." When you do that, you will discover that as a subject of His kingdom, you will know peace as you have never known it.

Today Can Be Different

Taking the Longer View

But Joseph said to them: ". . . You intended
to harm me, but God intended it for good
to accomplish what is now being done,
the saving of many lives."

GENESIS 50:19

*G*od can turn a bleak situation into one of redemp-
tive hope. When Joseph revealed his true identity
to his brothers, they were gripped with fear. After all,
as Governor of Egypt, he was now in a position to take
revenge for the wrong they did to him. Joseph, however, reassured them, "Don't be afraid. Am I in the place
of God? You intended to harm me, but God intended
it for good to accomplish what is now being done, the
saving of many lives" (Genesis 50:19–20).

When you think that everything is against you and
that God has forgotten you, go back and read the story
of Joseph's life. Then realize that sometimes only the
perspective of time will help you understand that God
was with you all the time! You just didn't know. It's what
we don't know that must be taken by faith.

365 Guidelines for Daily Living

He is Lord!

Therefore I make known to you that no one speaking by the Spirit of God calls Jesus accursed and no one can say that Jesus is Lord except by the Holy Spirit.

1 CORINTHIANS 12:3 NKJV

Many great hymns talk about Jesus Christ as Lord. We sing "The Church's one foundation is Jesus Christ our Lord" or "He is Lord, He is risen from the dead and He is Lord." Yet sometimes we sing phrases without really knowing what they mean.

When the disciples called Jesus "Lord," they meant more than the equivalent of "Sir." They understood that to call Jesus "Lord" meant they recognized Him as God. How do we know this? It was one of the reasons the Pharisees became so enraged! They didn't mind the disciples calling Jesus "Sir" but to recognize Him as God enraged them.

In fact, the disciples never called Christ by His personal name "Jesus" in the gospel accounts. For three years they walked with Him and saw Him do things no mortal man could do. They knew He was not just a "perfect man," for no human could awaken the dead, cause the blind to see, or heal deaf ears. Finally, the Resurrection showed them that Jesus Christ was not simply the Savior, He was Lord!

Is He your Lord?

Today Can Be Different

Worrying about Failure

*And whatever you do, whether in word or deed,
do it all in the name of the Lord Jesus, giving
thanks to God the Father through him.*

COLOSSIANS 3:17

Some folks are so concerned about failing that they never even try. They never leave the familiar to test uncharted waters. Content with mediocrity, they refuse to gamble with the possibility of loss, not understanding that it often takes failures to produce success.

R.H. Macy, the man who founded the famous American department store chain Macy's, went through seven business failures before he succeeded. No one remembers the bankruptcy of Walt Disney before he succeeded. Who recalls that Babe Ruth, the all-time hero of baseball, struck out a record 1,330 times at bat? He's remembered for his 714 home runs.

Age, social standing, and education have little to do with success. Rather, it is that indefinable burning desire to succeed, to give it your best shot, that separates those who accomplish things from those who never really try.

"Whatever you do," says Paul, "work at it with all your heart." Only the person who does nothing makes no mistakes, and neither does he or she succeed.

365 Guidelines for Daily Living

Awesome

Much dreaming and many words are meaning-less. Therefore, stand in awe of God.

ECCLESIASTES 5:7

Solomon, known as the wisest man in the world, said we should stand in awe of God (Ecclesiastes 5:7).

If one word could even come close to describing the Almighty, the One who spoke the Word and brought the world into existence, it would be the word awesome. What a marvelous, great God we serve!

When we stand in awe of God, we will neither take Him for granted nor assume that we can violate what He says in His Word and not face the consequences of our actions. We approach Him with an attitude of wonder and reverence.

There are many facets to the truth that God is an awesome God. Don't learn about Him just intellectually. Know Him personally and experientially. The more you know of Him, the more you will realize your own weaknesses and inadequacies. Solomon was right, awesome is the perfect word to describe our mighty God.

Today Can Be the Best Day of Your Life

Anchors

*They cast four anchors out of the stern,
and wished for the day.*

ACTS 27:29

When the winds of life blow, unless we have anchors that hold us, the fragile ship of our lives may crash against the rocks.

When the storms of life rage, you need four anchors: faith in God, faith in yourself, faith in your family, and faith in your friends. But there are times when your friends fail you, when your family lets you down, when you can hardly believe in yourself. Only the anchor of faith in God endures when everything else fails.

The writer of Hebrews talked about things that change in life, but then, speaking of God's promises, he said, "We have this hope as an anchor for the soul, firm and secure" (Hebrews 6:19). This hope is anchored to the Rock of Ages.

Raging storms are one thing; subtle currents that catch you unaware are another. With the storm, you've got to fight to stay alive. But with the subtle currents you don't know what's happening. Subtle currents can pull your boat without you knowing it until you realize you are already a long way from where you are supposed to be. In either case, make sure your anchor holds.

Today Can Be the Best Day of Your Life

Gratitude

*But I will sacrifice to You with the voice
of thanksgiving.*

JONAH 2:9 NKJV

Gratitude," wrote L. R. Akers, "has been called the memory of the heart. A heart without gratitude is like a grate filled with fuel but unlighted; a cold and dead thing. A cardinal sin of our modern life is ingratitude."

Our first obligation of gratitude is to God. Bowing our heads to thank Him for our food is one sign of gratitude. Christ gave us an example of this when He "took the seven loaves and the fish, and when he had given thanks, he broke them and gave them to the disciples, and they in turn to the people" (Matthew 15:36).

Gratitude involves giving rather than receiving. On one occasion, Christ healed ten lepers, yet only one came back to express his appreciation. Too often, we are like the nine other lepers. God answers our prayer, He meets our needs, He undertakes on our behalf; and we go merrily along our own way, never stopping to express our gratitude to Him.

Gratitude is oil to the machinery of life. The man who *thinks* is a man who *thanks*.

Today Can Be Different

Thankful for Everything

*Be joyful always; pray continually; give thanks
in all circumstances, for this is God's will for you
in Christ Jesus.*

1 THESSALONIANS 5:16-18

*P*aul advised us always to be joyful, always to pray,
and always to give thanks.

Notice that Paul doesn't say, "Thank God for everything that happens to you," but rather, "in every situation." In every circumstance thank God for He is able to redeem the difficulty and help you come out on the other side with rejoicing.

It is attitude that makes the difference. It is acknowledging that no matter how dark the clouds, there is a silver lining; that every dark valley has a way out; that every night is followed by a dawn; and that everything, except eternity, will eventually be over.

Ingratitude was one of the major sins of those whom God eventually allowed to suffer in their foolishness. Paul wrote, "For although they knew God, they neither glorified him as God nor gave thanks to him, but their thinking became futile and their foolish hearts were darkened" (Romans 1:21).

Take time to reflect on 1 Thessalonians 5, and use it as a benchmark to check your attitude. Paul was right on target when he said, "In everything give thanks."

Today Can Be the Best Day of Your Life

Thanksgiving (1)

Let us come before Him with thanksgiving and extol Him with music and song. For the LORD is the great God, the great King above all gods.

PSALM 95:2–3

The custom of a special day or period of thanksgiving was initiated by God Himself when He instructed ancient Israel to set aside a week of festivities in gratitude for the harvest He had provided.

Known as the Feast of the Harvest, it was a time of rejoicing and giving thanks for the rain and sunshine that brought the harvest. The event was corporate, yet it was personal as each individual reflected on the source of his blessings. Each day during the feast work came to a halt, and people took the time to turn their thoughts toward God.

Some say we are a thankless people today. Ingratitude is often linked to the sin of busyness even more than the sin of indifference. It is often the result of our failing to take time to count our blessings. Yes, there is much in life that brings hardship, yet thanksgiving does not mean that we reflect on what's wrong in our lives. Rather, giving thanks to God makes us focus on what's right in a broken, imperfect world. For God's blessings—not man's failures—we give thanks.

Today Can Be the Best Day of Your Life

Thanksgiving (2)

*I will praise the name of God with song, and shall
magnify Him with thanksgiving.*

PSALM 69:30 NASB

A man who knew what it was to be imprisoned
unjustly, to be beaten and left for dead, to face
one trial after another on trumped-up charges, wrote
this to his friends: "In everything give thanks; for this
is God's will for you in Christ Jesus" (1 Thessalonians
5:18 NASB). The man was the Apostle Paul.

Paul had learned that the circumstances of life are
not permanent. "The things which are seen are tempo-
ral, but the things which are not seen are eternal"
(2 Corinthians 4:18 NASB). He looked at life from a
different perspective. He saw life not as an opportunity to amass fortune or to be well-liked by his contem-
poraries, but to serve Christ. Thus he said, "I have been
crucified with Christ; and it is no longer I who live, but
Christ lives in me; and the life which I now live in the
flesh I live by faith in the Son of God, who loved me,
and delivered Himself up for me" (Galatians 2:20).

You have a choice: You can hang your head in
defeat, or you can lift your heart and voice toward
heaven and praise the Lord.

Today Can Be Different

Faith and Trust

May the Lord reward your work, and your wages be full from the LORD, the God of Israel, under whose wings you have come to seek refuge.

RUTH 2:12

a century ago John Stockton wrote a song, part of which goes: "Only trust Him now; He will save you, He will save you now." Following the advice of Stockton is not always easy. It's easier to trust our resources, our skills, our knowledge; we would even rather gamble with the odds than simply trust God.

Here are three simple guidelines that can help you trust God more.

GUIDELINE 1: Stretch the muscle of your faith. Has God ever answered a prayer for you? I'm certain you can single out at least one time when what you prayed for was granted. Remember how God has already answered your prayers, then be encouraged by the truth that He will provide for your needs today.

GUIDELINE 2: Be encouraged by the testimonies of others. God does not show favoritism (see Romans 2:11; Ephesians 6:9; Colossians 3:25). If you want to build your faith, then talk to those whose prayers have been heard.

GUIDELINE 3: If you want to know how to trust God more, stand on the assurance of His Word.

May God help us to trust Him more today.

Today Can Be Different

Homeward Bound

*Now we know that if the earthly tent we live
in is destroyed, we have a building from God,
an eternal house in heaven, not built by
human hands.*

2 CORINTHIANS 5:1

Walking around the house we had lived in for the
last twenty years, I couldn't help but become
emotional. After two decades, we reluctantly decided
the time had come to move.

I couldn't help remembering the dinners we had
with our parents and friends, most of whom are now
in heaven, the years our children grew up, times of
celebrations, and the noise of everyone trying to talk
at once.

The furniture were gone. The floor was swept clean.
The rooms were empty. Right now, we're awaiting the
completion of a new house. The closer we get to being
able to move in and get settled, the less we think about
the memories of what we left behind. Then I got to
thinking about heaven. The closer we get to it, the more
there's a pull—something which tugs at the heart and
blurs the thoughts of what is left behind. Ah, yes, focus
on heaven.

365 Guidelines for Daily Living

Taking the Path Less Traveled

What good is it for a man to gain the whole world, yet forfeit his soul?

MARK 8:36

The English word "integrity" comes from a word that means "uprightness." Often, integrity is neither appreciated nor rewarded. Doing the right thing because you might be rewarded isn't true integrity. Integrity means doing the right thing simply because it's the right thing to do.

I've spent a lot of time in both former and present Communist countries where God has largely been left out of life's equation. I've come to the conclusion that integrity is part of the moral fabric of a society if it recognizes its ultimate accountability to God. Honoring God makes me accountable to you as my neighbor or friend.

Doing right only when it is rewarded creates a Pavlovian response. But when we are motivated by integrity, we do the right thing because our conscience demands it. The quick fix, the shortcut, the feeling that we can get away with something that feels good or is profitable is what drives societies to moral bankruptcy. The pathway of integrity is the one that honors God.

Tomorrow Can Be Beautiful

Listen to God's Voice

No one knows about that day or hour, not even the angels in heaven, nor the Son, but only the Father.

MATTHEW 24:36

One sign that is connected with Christ's return is earthquakes. No matter how Bible scholars may disagree on other issues, they generally agree that the increase of earthquakes in our world is one of the signs pointing to His return.

God said in Joel 2:30–31, "I will show wonders in the heavens and on the earth, blood and fire and billows of smoke. The sun will be turned to darkness and the moon to blood before the coming of the great and dreadful day of the LORD."

Listen to God's voice—whether it is in earthquakes, in the beauty of a sunrise, or in the miracle of a baby's birth. Sometimes His voice is quiet like a whisper. Occasionally, He may raise the volume to get your attention. God speaks clearly through His Word, but He gets our attention through the events of life. Yes, listen to His voice.

Today Can Be the Best Day of Your Life

December

Today in the town of David
a Savior has been born to you;
he is Christ the Lord.

LUKE 2:11

It's December Again!

But when the time had fully come, God sent His Son.

GALATIANS 4:4

It's December 1 and Christmas is only twenty-four days away. Suppose this Christmas season, we decide to do things differently. Two simple words can make the difference: Plan ahead! Get out your calendar and do some strategic planning. Consider some of the following ideas:

IDEA 1: Adopt a needy family this Christmas.

IDEA 2: Have your kids prepare a gift for a needy child.

IDEA 3: Do something for someone that requires an emotional connection, not just an act of charity.

IDEA 4: Evaluate your shopping and spending. An amazing amount of money is spent out of guilt.

IDEA 5: Plan a birthday party for Jesus. You would be amazed at the number of people who do not connect the birth of Jesus Christ with December 25.

All these ideas require planning, which is why I'm prompting you to make the days count and to make this Christmas the most meaningful one of your life. Remember, Christmas involves giving—not receiving.

Tomorrow Begins Today

When God Collides with Circumstances

*I am the LORD, the God of all mankind.
Is anything too hard for me?*

JEREMIAH 32:27

Do you believe that "man's extremity is God's opportunity"? Scores of people have discovered that when they got to the end of their rope, when there's nowhere left to go, there they found God.

On two occasions God asked this question of man, "Is anything too hard for Me?" The obvious answer is "No!" The first time God asked the question, He had just promised a baby to a ninety-year old woman.

The second time God asked this question, He had told Jeremiah to go out and buy property at a time when the nation was about to be overthrown. God promised that after seventy years of captivity He would bring His people back to the land. Jeremiah's getting a corner on the real estate market was proof of his faith in God's ability and faithfulness to do what He promised. God asked, "I am the LORD, the God of all mankind. Is anything too hard for me?" (Jeremiah 32:27).

Do not measure God by the gravity of your circumstances, rather, measure your circumstances by the might of His power.

365 Guidelines for Daily Living

Get to Know God

Now this is eternal life: that they may know You, the only true God, and Jesus Christ, whom You have sent.

JOHN 17:3

If you were to interview God, what would you ask Him? "Why is there suffering in our world?" "Why don't You strike down the wicked and eliminate the evil in our world?" "Why must a childless woman desperately wish for a baby when thousands of children are aborted every year?" "Why do You allow strife and wars?" Supposing you got an answer to your questions, would you really understand? Probably not.

Conducting an interview consists of asking questions and recording answers. Beyond that, there's no personal involvement. An interview and a relationship don't have the same degree of involvement and intimacy. Knowing about God—which few people really do—is only the beginning. Knowing God involves a relationship of communication, interaction, and commitment. Why is knowing God important? Only when you know God will you love Him. Only when you love God will you obey Him.

Get to know God. It's the most important knowledge you will ever have, and an absolute necessity if you intend to spend eternity in His presence.

Tomorrow Can Be Beautiful

Our Incredible Universe

The heavens declare the glory of God; the skies proclaim the work of his hands.

PSALM 19:1

Anyone who has ever looked at the stars on a dark night has been awestruck by the vastness and greatness of space, yet only several men in history have been privileged to stand on the moon and look back towards the Blue Planet, as Earth has been described. When astronaut Jim Irwin stood on the surface of the moon, the earth was 239,000 miles away. Jim said that from that distance, the Earth appeared to be the size of a walnut.

God did not simply create the Earth, bringing our world into existence out of nothing. He also demonstrated His love for our Earth by sending His Son to be born of a woman—flesh and blood as we are —understanding our temptations, our heartaches, our brokenness, our frustrations.

God is not out there, far away beyond the most distant galaxy. He is as close as your need, and He reveals something of that personal care for you as you trust Him. He's the God who cares as well as the God who created.

365 Guidelines for Daily Living

Belief and Trust

For I am confident of this very thing, that He who began a good work in you will perfect it until the day of Christ Jesus.

PHILIPPIANS 1:6 NASB

In her excellent book *The Secret of a Happy Christian Life*, Hannah Whitall Smith, wrote, "Faith is the simplest and plainest thing in the world . . . it is simply believing God."

Real faith consists of two elements: belief, which appeals to the mind; and trust, which is experiential and demands a response to what you believe.

We believe God can do the things we are hoping for, but we don't think He will. Belief we have; but we're short on trust, and without trust our faith is incomplete. Trust is the assurance that God, who cannot lie, will never let you down. Trust is faith in action, rest from your anxious striving, freedom from worry, and surrender to the will of a loving heavenly Father—confident that God is fully in control.

How would you define your faith? Is it belief alone? Or is it a belief that knows you can trust God to do what He says? You can rest in that kind of faith—no, actually, you can rest in that kind of God!

Today Can Be Different

The Futility of Worry

Indeed, he who watches over Israel will neither slumber nor sleep.

PSALM 121:4

Here is a list of suggestions to help you fight worry: First, confront your problem. Worrying about cancer does not make it go away, neither does it give you peace of mind. It won't make you better-looking or solve your financial problems. Confronting the problem is the first positive step towards a solution.

Second, challenge your problem. If you can do something about it, do it. You will then find that your mind is filled with thoughts of positive action rather than needless worry.

Third, commit your worry to God. God's providence and watchful care will solve the problems which you cannot solve by yourself.

Look at the lilies that bloom, and the blades of grass and remember who takes care of them. Notice the little bird that builds his nest in a giant tree, then ponder the question that Christ asked His disciples, "Are you not much more valuable than they?" (Matthew 6:26). Worry does not rob tomorrow of troubles; it only takes the joy from today.

365 Guidelines for Daily Living

Discipleship

Whoever finds his life will lose it, and whoever loses his life for my sake will find it.

MATTHEW 10:39

What measures a real disciple of Jesus Christ? When the Communists took over China, Sam Moffatt was arrested and thrown into prison. One day, thinking of the turmoil that had come to that country and of his own fate, he asked one of his captors, "What chance is there?" The man replied, "None." "Why?" asked Moffatt. "Because we are willing to die for what we believe, and I do not believe you are."

The crosses that we bear today are made of 24K gold. The significance of the Cross has been reduced to an adornment we wear around our necks. But the Cross demands commitment—not consideration! Christ asks us no less today than He did 2,000 years ago. It will take the same price if our generation is to be reached with the message of the gospel—the price the disciples were willing to pay—everything!

When Charles Lindberg decided to fly the Atlantic, waters that no other had successfully crossed, he drew a line on his map which he called the "Point of No Return." After he crossed that point, Lindberg knew there was no turning back, and so it is with the one who means business in following Jesus Christ.

Today Can Be Different

If Only

In the morning you will say, "If only it were evening!" and in the evening, "If only it were morning!"

DEUTERONOMY 28:67

*H*ave you ever caught yourself looking back, regretting an unfortunate decision? "If only I had not done that." "If only I had said no!" There is an "if only" for every mistake you have made.

Almost everyone gives in to the urge to say, "if only." But when you dwell on the past, you live in a world of broken pieces, frustrations and defeat. What happened is history and cannot be changed.

There are two words that can make all the difference. Instead of dwelling on "if onlys," accept the consequences and look to a brighter future by adding the words "and yet."

Joseph was sold into slavery by his brothers. He could have easily lived in a world of broken dreams. But Joseph majored on the "and yets." He believed God could take a failure and turn it into a victory.

Are you tempted to dwell on the past saying, "If only"? When you say, 'If only," you despair of God's bringing good out of a difficult situation. "And yet" helps you focus on what God can yet bring out of a tough one.

Today Can Be Different

The Woman at Sychar

Whoever drinks of the water that I will give him shall never thirst; but the water that I will give him will become in him a well of water springing up to eternal life.

JOHN 4:14 NASB

She was surprised when the stranger spoke to her so her response was carefully weighed. The woman wasn't a stranger to men, though. If anyone knew about broken relationships, she did. Married five times and divorced the same number, she was despairing of ever having a good relationship with anyone.

There were lots of reasons why Jesus should have pulled away and rejected her, but He reached across the barriers that separate people from Him. He said, "If you drink of the water that I give, you will never thirst again."

Do you see yourself in the heart of this Samaritan woman? Are you frustrated by relationships, hurt by people who said they loved you but rejected you?

If you are willing to reach out to Jesus, you'll discover that Jesus will reveal Himself as Christ. What follows will be a relationship with the One who will never disappoint you. Jesus will meet your deepest needs.

Today Can Be Different

Courage

We are hard pressed on every side, but not crushed; perplexed, but not in despair; persecuted, but not abandoned; struck down, but not destroyed.

2 CORINTHIANS 4:8-9

When it comes to courage, you cannot chart it. When it is displayed, a person is seen as a hero, and when it is missing, a person is called a coward.

Courage is what Elijah had when he stormed into the presence of the king and said, "As the LORD, the God of Israel, lives, whom I serve, there will be neither dew nor rain in the next few years except at my word" (1 Kings 17:1). Courage is what Daniel had when he threw open his windows and prayed three times a day, even though the king had passed a law forbidding prayer.

Men and women today must find courage to speak their convictions, to stand for what is right and to abide by godly principles. Individuals who are courageous often pay a price for their courage. But real courage does not consider the cost; it considers only the rightness of the action that must be taken.

Where do you get courage? Paul said, "If God is for us, who can be against us?" (Romans 8:31). Like any man who stands courageously for a cause, Paul experienced trouble; yet, he still stood boldly for what he believed in. You can too, as you thank God and take courage.

Today Can Be the Best Day of Your Life

Choosing Your Response to Suffering

And we know that in all things God works for the good of those who love Him, who have been called according to His purpose.

ROMANS 8:28

What you believe about God shapes your attitude toward suffering.

How well we respond to difficulties is usually the measure of how well we know God's Word. For those whose knowledge is based on misconceptions, depression and anger result. They feel that God has failed them. But for those who know the Word, there's a deeper trust in God and an understanding of suffering.

When Joseph confronted his brothers who had sold him into slavery, he said, "You meant it for evil, but God meant it for good." Because our human vision is limited, we cannot see how good can come from evil. That's where the power of faith—tried by pain and suffering—makes the difference.

Sometimes we can see the rhyme and reason of difficult or tough times. However, some situations defy human logic, where asking the question, "Why?" is only an exercise in futility. Someday we might know why, but by then, perhaps, it just won't matter.

Tomorrow Begins Today

Perfect—the Enemy of Good

Don't copy the behavior and customs of this world, but be a new and different person with a fresh newness in all you do and think.

ROMANS 12:2 TLB

My family owes a debt of gratitude to Dr. John James, a children's surgeon who pioneered a radical approach to helping babies who would otherwise be deformed. Dr. James's surgical brilliance helped my little grandson's head to look normal when the bones on his head did not separate as they normally do before birth.

Another doctor suggested further surgery but Dr. James opted against it saying, "Perfect is the enemy of good." He explained that while surgery was necessary the first time, further surgery, in the quest for perfection, would carry greater risks than benefits.

Being committed to excellence is one thing, but being obsessed with perfection is something else. Has our generation been so hyped by the glitz of the perfect figure and the perfect face that we have lost sight of the importance of being authentic?

Who says you need perfection? The madness that demands perfection is neither godly nor realistic.

Today Can Be the Best Day of Your Life

The Upside of Doubt

O God, you are my God, earnestly I seek you;
my soul thirsts for you, my body longs for you,
in a dry and weary land where there is no water.
PSALM 63:1

What's good about doubt? Consider these five observations:

- It is better to deal with doubt and search for what you believe than to live with doubt and never know what you believe.

- It is better to doubt your faith than for you to believe your doubt.

- It is better to confront truth that will survive testing than to never question what is untrue.

- It is better to take your doubts to the Lord than to let your doubts take you from the Lord.

- It is better to act on what you know to be true than to be paralyzed by your doubt.

Act on your faith. What we don't understand begins to fade as our foundation of faith strengthens. In this side of heaven, nobody ever has all the answers. Don't let doubt stop you. God never reproves those who doubt their faith, but He does censure those who refuse to believe. There is a big difference.

365 Guidelines for Daily Living

Do You Read Your Bible?

*I rejoice at Your word as one who finds
great treasure.*

PSALM 119:162 NKJV

I was standing inside a Buddhist temple in Guangzhou, China when a young university student approached a member of our group to practice his English. After a few minutes of conversation, the student asked, "Do you have a Bible?"

The tourist replied, "Not with me, but I have one at home." "Do you read it?" asked the student. The tourist candidly replied, "No, not much, but it's there . . ." Puzzled, the Chinese young man queried, "If you have a Bible, why do you not read it?"

This was no set-up political interrogation but the searching of a young man who had been denied religious freedom all his life. He could not understand how someone could possess something so precious as a Bible and not read it, let alone study or memorize it.

The Bible is not like an amulet or charm that brings luck to the owner. Rather, it is a textbook on living; a road map that will take you by the foot of the Cross to heaven's shore. Do not just possess a Bible; let it possess you.

Today Can Be the Best Day of Your Life

Inferiority

We are God's workmanship, created in Christ
Jesus to do good works.

EPHESIANS 2:10

*W*e all know what it's like to feel inferior, but what causes these feelings? Feelings of inferiority usually stem from three sources: worry, guilt and anger. A person who worries can be paralyzed by his own fears. Feeling guilty for actions or attitudes makes us wonder if something is wrong with us. Bursts of anger make us feel inadequate and inferior to others.

In the Bible, God shows us how to find His power. God certainly did not say you were inferior. You are as important to God as anyone else. What God has done for others He will do for you.

If you have trusted Jesus as your Lord and Savior, your life does not go on according to chance. God has directed your life so that you may accomplish His work. When you are plagued by inferiority, commit yourself to the Lord. Ask Him for strength. Then roll up your sleeves and go to work. Who said you were inferior? Forget it, and do the job God has for you to do today.

Today Can Be the Best Day of Your Life

God Knows

"For I know the plans that I have for you,"
declares the Lord, "plans for welfare and not for
calamity to give you a future and a hope."
JEREMIAH 29:11 NASB

In times of difficulty or disaster, nothing is more comforting than meeting someone who knows how to help you. God's people found themselves in a no-way out situation during Jeremiah's day.

God saw their tears, felt their frustration, and responded saying, "'For I know the plans that I have for you,' declares the Lord, 'plans for welfare and not for calamity to give you a future and a hope'" (Jeremiah 29:11 NASB).

You may be thinking, "How can God bring any order out of the chaos of my life?" Don't worry; that's His problem, not yours. If God has a plan (and He does), then His plan has to be better than yours because He knows the end from the beginning.

Following that great promise, God said, "Then you will call upon Me and come and pray to Me, and I will listen to you. You will seek Me and find Me, when you search for Me with all your heart" (Jeremiah 29:12–13 NASB). Seek the Lord with all your heart. That is the answer.

Tomorrow Begins Today

Give Thanks

For even though they knew God, they did not honor Him as God, or give thanks; but they became futile in their speculations, and their foolish heart was darkened.

ROMANS 1:21 NASB

The note to the dentist, written in a child's hand, read, "Dear Dr., Thank you very much for the retainer. My dad told me how thankful I should be and I am. I did not really want a retainer, but I know it will help me and make my teeth grow straight. My dad told me to take very good care of it. This gift is the biggest gift I have ever got, and it probably will be the biggest gift I ever do get. Love, Bethel."

Often we are grateful but don't take time to express our gratitude. Perhaps we just assume that someone knows we appreciate what he or she did, so we don't make the effort to write a note or make a phone call or say thanks in person.

To whom do you owe gratitude—teachers, parents, career mentors, neighbors, Sunday school teachers, friends? No one is self-made. You are where you are now because someone, somewhere, helped you along the way.

"In everything give thanks, for this is God's will for you in Christ Jesus" (1 Thessalonians 5:18 NASB).

Today Can Be Different

Forgiving Yourself (1)

But there is forgiveness with thee, that thou mayest be feared.

PSALM 130:4 KJV

*M*any today, not understanding the nature of God's forgiveness, live lives full of frustration and self-condemnation. A man wrote, "I have a wonderful family: wife, three boys and one daughter, all saved, yet I am so miserable. I just cannot forgive myself for . . . ." He then mentioned something that happened years ago.

God's forgiveness is based on His nature and character. God promises to forgive us provided we turn from our sin to the Savior and confess our need for forgiveness.

Learning to forgive oneself is one of the most difficult tasks that confronts a person, but it's possible. The first step to forgiving ourselves is to acknowledge the fullness of God's forgiveness.

365 Guidelines for Daily Living

Forgiving Yourself (2)

I . . . will not remember thy sins.

ISAIAH 43:25 KJV

*G*od has forgiven me, but I just cannot forgive myself." The following guidelines will guide you how to forgive yourself—once and for all:

GUIDELINE 1: Claim God's promise that He will forgive your sins. Get your Bible and mark passages on forgiveness such Isaiah 43:25 which says, "I, even I, am he who blots out your transgressions, for my own sake, and remembers sins no more."

GUIDELINE 2: Confess your sin once and for all. Stop insulting God by asking Him to forgive you of the same thing day after day.

GUIDELINE 3: Thank God for His forgiveness. "But I do not feel anything," you might say. A lot of people pour out their hearts in scalding confession, then feel great. Then after a few days, the guilt they felt comes back and they do not feel that God has heard them. The promises of God are true not because we feel something; they are true because of the nature and character of God.

GUIDELINE 4: Refuse to let your mind dwell on that which was already forgiven by God.

His forgiveness forever cancels out the deed. You *can* forgive yourself, today.

365 Guidelines for Daily Living

Admitting Your Weakness

My grace is sufficient for you, for my power is made perfect in weakness.

2 CORINTHIANS 12:9

Three men were discussing their greatest weaknesses. The first said he was unable to resist alcohol. The second said, "I can't control the videos I watch." The third man only nodded. Finally, with a sheepish smile, he said, "My problem is, I can't resist gossiping, and right now I can't wait to get out of here."

What does God say about our flaws? Sometimes we wish He'd just ignore them, but that isn't what the Bible says. God knows our weaknesses, and the Bible says we're responsible for our failures. God doesn't say, "Poor fellow, he can't help it; he's only human," what He says is, "My strength is made perfect in weakness."

When you admit your weakness and allow God to touch your life, His strength begins to reinforce your resolve to do right. Instead of being defeated time and again, you'll see God's Holy Spirit give you the strength you need to do the right thing.

God never forces Himself on you. But when you say, "Lord, fill and heal my weakness," He goes to work and meets your need.

Tomorrow Begins Today

When You Are Taken Captive by Trouble

When you pass through the waters, I will be with you; and when you pass through the rivers, they will not sweep over you. . . . For I am the LORD, your God, the Holy One of Israel, your Savior. . . .

ISAIAH 43:2-3

I shall never forget a conversation I had with Wang Ming Dao, the father of the Chinese House Church Movement, shortly before his death. This saintly man had been in prison for twenty-two years at the hands of the Communists who banned religion in China.

In his book *A Stone Made Smooth*, Wang explains how God uses difficulty to polish our lives, like water polishes stone in a riverbed. "Brother Wang," I said, "many years ago I read your book." He smiled and quickly responded, "Stone still not yet smooth." Though well into his 80s, this godly man knew that God was still polishing his stone.

By our human understanding, there is no rhyme or reason why God allows us to face the tough hours, but I am certain that He keeps working in our lives in order to refine us.

Tomorrow Can Be Beautiful

Soar Like an Eagle

*Saul and Jonathan—in life they were loved and
gracious, and in death they were not parted.
They were swifter than eagles, they were stronger
than lions.*

2 SAMUEL 1:23

When eagles take to the air their wings stretch out
up to seven feet across, their feathers spread out
in a curtain, catching the wind currents high above the
ground. Eagles don't fly; they soar.

Isaiah says that "those who hope in the Lord will
renew their strength. They will soar on wings like
eagles; they will run and not grow weary, they will walk
and not be faint" (Isaiah 40:31). Isaiah uses three levels
of movement to illustrate his point: walking, running,
and soaring like an eagle. If you are to rise above the
gravitational pull of so much in life, soaring as an eagle,
you must place your hope and your life in the Lord.

When you make the decision to let God's Spirit
guide you, you will begin to gain spiritual altitude.

Don't be content to live a sparrow's existence when
you could soar like an eagle.

Tomorrow Begins Today

When Nothing Seems to be Happening

The angel said to them, "Do not be afraid. I bring you good news of great joy that will be for all the people. Today in the town of David a Savior has been born to you; he is Christ the Lord."

LUKE 2:10-11

After Jesus' birth, Mary and Joseph took Him and hid in Egypt for two years. Later they returned to Nazareth, where Jesus grew up. At age thirty, He went to the synagogue at Nazareth and read a selection from Isaiah, which read, "The Spirit of the Lord is on me, because He has anointed me to preach good news to the poor. He has sent me to proclaim freedom for the prisoners and recovery of sight for the blind, to release the oppressed, to proclaim the year of the Lord's favor" (Luke 4:18–19).

He never studied in a university, yet He knew people better than they knew themselves. He healed the sick with a word. He touched blind eyes, and they saw. He opened deaf ears, and they heard. He merely gave the command and it took place.

This year, rethink Christmas. Go beyond the veneer, and discover what really happened when the world thought nothing was happening.

Today Can Be the Best Day of Your Life

Experiencing the Glory of Christmas

We have seen his glory, the glory of the one and only Son, who came from the Father, full of grace and truth.

JOHN 1:14

Some things are better encountered than explained. So it is with the glory of God.

When sinful man encounters the Almighty and His glory, his life will never be the same. The shepherds who experienced the glory of that first Christmas came and worshiped the Child who had been born in Bethlehem. They then spread the word that God had sent a Savior in the person of the Child born that night in a stable.

The difference between the glory of God and our human concept of glory is that God's glory is vitally connected with His person and His attributes. When Isaiah had a marvelous encounter with God and saw the glory of God, he heard the seraphim cry out, "Holy, holy, holy is the Lord Almighty; the whole earth is full of his glory" (Isaiah 6:3).

Want to see the glory of God? Look in the pages of the Bible and ask God to touch your life with His glory. Come to Him with expectancy and faith, and you will find that your life will never be the same.

Today Can Be the Best Day of Your Life

The Ten Wonders of Christmas

But [Christ] emptied Himself, taking the form of a bond-servant . . . and being made in the likeness of men.

PHILIPPIANS 2:7 NASB

Over 365 names are found in the Bible referring to Jesus Christ, but none is lovelier than the one in Isaiah: "His name shall be called Wonderful" (9:6 KJV).

First, there is the wonder of *His birth*.

Second, there's the wonder of *His condescension*.

Third, is the wonder of *His character*.

Fourth, is the wonder of *His person*.

Fifth, is the wonder of *His words*.

Sixth, is the wonder of *His works*.

Seventh, is the wonder of *His death*.

Eighth, is the wonder of *His resurrection*.

Ninth, is the wonder of *His second coming*.

Last, is the wonder of *His saving power*. "For He shall save His people from their sins" (Matthew 1:21 KJV).

Today Can Be Different

The Day after Christmas

And surely I will be with you always, to the very end of the age.

MATTHEW 28:20

Christmas Day is over. But today there's good news no matter where you are, and no matter how you feel. The coming of Jesus Christ to our earth which we celebrated yesterday has an abiding importance even on the day after Christmas—and the day after that, and the week after that.

His presence is not merely an emotional or psychological upper. It touches the depths of your being. G. Campbell Morgan once read the words of Jesus in Matthew 28:20 to an elderly woman on her deathbed. He said to her, "Isn't that a wonderful promise?" "Sir," replied the woman, "that isn't a promise—it's a fact!"

Be encouraged, no matter where you are—no matter how you feel on this day after Christmas—there is one who cares for you deeply. Christmas may be over, but His promise is with us forever: "Lo, I am with you always, even to the end of the age" (Matthew 28:20 NASB).

Today Can Be Different

Multi-Tasking

*Forgetting what is behind and straining toward
what is ahead, I press on toward the goal to win
the prize for which God has called me heavenward in Christ Jesus.*

PHILIPPIANS 3:13-14

The word "multi-tasking" can only be found in the most recent dictionaries, but chances are good that you're familiar with the concept.

Kevin Maney defines multi-tasking as "doing as many things simultaneously as possible." Brushing your teeth at the same time you put on your shoes and listen to the morning news would qualify. Or driving and talking on your cell phone at the same time.

As I watch women driving to work while putting on their makeup or curling their lashes, and men shaving while downing a mug of coffee, I'm inclined to think that chatting with a friend, or playing ball with your son, or walking with your daughter on the beach might be far more productive in the long haul than winning a medal for multi-tasking. Only you can decide how to keep the main thing the main thing.

Tomorrow Can Be Beautiful

Touched by His Glory

An angel of the Lord appeared to them, and the glory of the Lord shone around them.

LUKE 2:9

$\mathcal{A}$ny real encounter with God would have to include the glory of God. Do you remember the experience of the shepherds in the fields outside of Bethlehem when angels appeared and announced the birth of the coming Messiah?

When I think of the glory of God, especially relating to Christmas, I am reminded of the annual Christmas display at the Denver Dry Goods Store, in the city where I grew up. When I stood on my toes and pressed my face to the window, I could see only part of the display. My father would pick me up and hold me up so I could see more. Only then could I begin to see the vastness of that wonderful Christmas display.

The glory of God is much like that. With our human inadequacies, our vision is dimmed by the selfishness of our old nature. We can only begin to fathom the glory of God when the Holy Spirit opens our eyes to this marvelous encounter with the divine.

Today Can Be the Best Day of Your Life

The God of Jacob

Therefore, if anyone is in Christ, he is a new creation; the old has gone, the new has come! All this is from God, who reconciled us to himself through Christ and gave us the ministry of reconciliation.

2 CORINTHIANS 5:17–18

Learning to call on God when we make mistakes can be tough. Jacob had to go through some tough times before he learned that lesson. True, he got Esau's birthright, but he paid the price for fourteen years, living as a fugitive in a foreign land. Later Jacob himself became the victim of deceit as his favorite son, Joseph, was sold into slavery.

But there is good news! The grace of God is within reach of every person who realizes he is a deceiver, a fraud and a liar. It is often our failure that makes us reach toward God, who not only forgives but also touches our lives with His presence.

Take time to read Psalm 46, which begins, "God is our refuge and strength, an ever-present help in trouble." This psalm ends with the words, "The LORD Almighty is with us; the God of Jacob is our fortress." God is our fortress. He is also the refuge for all, even modern-day Jacobs. Yes, the God of Jacob is still our refuge!

Today Can Be the Best Day of Your Life

Transitions

*Do not be terrified; do not be discouraged,
for the LORD your God will be with you
wherever you go.*

JOSHUA 1:9

*T*ransitions in life are never easy. Remember how it was when you were a youngster and moved from one grade to another, or changed neighborhoods when your family moved? That same feeling arises as an adult when you move from one job to another. As you ponder the transition from one year to another, there's a trace of nostalgia, a hint of excitement and an element of fear.

Yet in the wise providence of God there comes a time when you have to close the door on one phase of your life and make the passage to the next. I noticed an interesting phrase found in the book of Acts where Luke used the phrase, "Now after these things were finished," where he tells how it was time for Paul to leave Ephesus and go to Jerusalem.

For some of you, tomorrow is a great big question mark and even acknowledging it creates fear in your heart. Reach out and take the strong hand of God and know He can walk with you day by day through the new year.

Today Can Be Different

A New Year is Upon Us

Conduct yourselves with wisdom toward outsiders,
making the most of the opportunity.

COLOSSIANS 4:5 NASB

*F*ormer British Prime Minister Lloyd George, was playing golf with a friend on one occasion when they had to cross a fenced area. His partner pushed the gate closed but did not bother to latch it. George, seeing the failure, went back and secured the gate. Then George told of an old doctor friend who lay dying. After calling his family and friends to his bedside, he gave these parting words, "Close every gate through which you have passed." Lloyd George said that he owed more to that bit of wisdom than to anything else he had ever heard.

To close the gate on yesterday's failure will require two things: God's forgiveness and your forgetfulness—His forgiveness and your willingness to close the gate.

The second part—your willingness to forgive yourself—is sometimes harder to do than to find God's forgiveness. Yet if God has given His Son to provide a way to forgive us, why should we do any less than to forgive ourselves?

Closing the gate on yesterday—and latching it—gives hope for tomorrow.

Today Can Be Different

If you would like to get in touch with the author, you can write to him at the following addresses:

In Asia

Dr. Harold Sala
GUIDELINES Philippines
Box 4000
Makati, Metro Manila
Philippines

In the United States

GUIDELINES INTERNATIONAL
Box G
Laguna Hills, CA 92654
Visit the GUIDELINES home page
www.guidelines.org
email: guidelines@guidelines.org

Other Books by Harold J. Sala

Connecting: 52 Guidelines
for Making Marriage Work

Joyfully Single in
a Couples' World

Raising Godly Kids:
52 Guidelines for
Counter-Culture Parenting

Successful Servants:
How God Uses Unlikely People
(booklet)

Touching God: 52 Guidelines
for Personal Prayer